Cambridge Elements

Elements in Gender and Politics
edited by
Tiffany D. Barnes
University of Texas at Austin
Diana Z. O'Brien
Washington University in St. Louis

LEGISLATING PEACE

How Gender Diverse Rebel Parties Encourage the Implementation of Gender Peace Agreement Provisions

Elizabeth L. Brannon
Indiana University Bloomington

Jakana Thomas
University of California San Diego

Shaftesbury Road, Cambridge CB2 8EA, United Kingdom

One Liberty Plaza, 20th Floor, New York, NY 10006, USA

477 Williamstown Road, Port Melbourne, VIC 3207, Australia

314–321, 3rd Floor, Plot 3, Splendor Forum, Jasola District Centre,
New Delhi – 110025, India

Cambridge University Press is part of Cambridge University Press & Assessment,
a department of the University of Cambridge.

We share the University's mission to contribute to society through the pursuit of
education, learning and research at the highest international levels of excellence.

www.cambridge.org
Information on this title: www.cambridge.org/9781009570848

DOI: 10.1017/9781009570862

© Elizabeth L. Brannon and Jakana Thomas 2026

This publication is in copyright. Subject to statutory exception and to the provisions
of relevant collective licensing agreements, no reproduction of any part may take
place without the written permission of Cambridge University Press & Assessment.

When citing this work, please include a reference to the DOI 10.1017/9781009570862

First published 2026

A catalogue record for this publication is available from the British Library

*A Cataloging-in-Publication data record for this Element is available from the Library
of Congress*

ISBN 978-1-009-57084-8 Hardback
ISBN 978-1-009-57087-9 Paperback
ISSN 2753-8117 (online)
ISSN 2753-8109 (print)

Additional resources for this publication at www.cambridge.org/Brannon.

Cambridge University Press & Assessment has no responsibility for the persistence
or accuracy of URLs for external or third-party internet websites referred to in this
publication and does not guarantee that any content on such websites is, or will remain,
accurate or appropriate.

For EU product safety concerns, contact us at Calle de José Abascal, 56, 1°, 28003
Madrid, Spain, or email eugpsr@cambridge.org

Legislating Peace

How Gender Diverse Rebel Parties Encourage the Implementation of Gender Peace Agreement Provisions

Elements in Gender and Politics

DOI: 10.1017/9781009570862
First published online: February 2026

Elizabeth L. Brannon
Indiana University Bloomington

Jakana Thomas
University of California San Diego

Author for correspondence: Elizabeth L. Brannon, librann@iu.edu

Abstract: Previous research demonstrates that women's participation in peace processes impacts the adoption of gendered peace provisions but leaves questions about whether women can also shape their implementation. Focusing specifically on the role of women elected to rebel parties, particularly those with experience as ex-rebels, this Element argues that women representatives encourage the implementation of gender provisions in peace agreements. It uses a novel dataset on the implementation of gender provisions in African peace agreements signed between 1990 and 2024 to test the relationship between women's political representation and the implementation of gender provisions. The authors supplement their statistical analyses with case evidence from Angola, Rwanda, and Colombia. They find that women's parliamentary representation, especially that of former rebels in rebel parties, has a positive effect on compliance with gender provisions. These findings contribute to the understanding of women's post-war political influence, the implementation of gendered peace provisions, and rebel party politics.

Keywords: peace processes, women's political representation, female rebels, rebel parties, peace implementation

© Elizabeth L. Brannon and Jakana Thomas 2026

ISBNs: 9781009570848 (HB), 9781009570879 (PB), 9781009570862 (OC)
ISSNs: 2753-8117 (online), 2753-8109 (print)

Contents

1	Introduction	1
2	Former Rebel Parties and the Implementation of Peace	12
3	The Implementation of Gender-Inclusive Provisions	19
4	Methodology	35
5	Statistical Results	52
6	Conclusion	74
	References	80

An Online Appendix for this Element is available at www.cambridge.org/Brannon

1 Introduction

In 1960, Frene Ginwala, a United Kingdom-trained lawyer, went into exile with hundreds of other African National Congress (ANC) activists after the South African government instituted a ban on the ANC and police killed scores of protesters during what became known as the Sharpeville Massacre. During her thirty years in exile, Ginwala became indispensable to the ANC; she helped develop secret routes to move ANC activists across the South African border, including Oliver Tambo and Nelson Mandela, and advanced key ANC party platforms, including the organization's position on gender equality. She also traveled around the globe, educating others on the organization's anti-apartheid struggle.[1] Ginwala returned to South Africa in 1990 when the ANC ban was lifted and took up a prominent role in the ANC Women's League. In this role, she pushed for women to be included in the negotiations to end apartheid and the subsequent transition process, and for women's interests to be integrated into the new constitution (Hassim 2002). She carried on these priorities after she was elected to parliament in 1994 and became the first speaker of the post-apartheid National Assembly. She repeatedly connected the empowerment and advancement of women to liberation priorities and prospects for a peaceful democratic transition (Geisler 2000).

Ginwala was not an aberration among former ANC activists. Women who participated in noncombat roles, like Ginwala, and those who participated in Umkhonto we Sizwe (MK), the ANC's armed wing, became mainstays in South African politics after the transition (Geisler 2000). Like Ginwala, many other female politicians from the ANC pushed for the fulfillment of the promises made to women throughout the war and in the negotiated settlement. Fearing their marginalization from post-conflict political discussions and opportunities (Geisler 2000), female former ANC members mobilized, contested in spaces from which they had been excluded, and advocated for the implementation of gendered policies every step of the way (Waylen 2014). This work extended beyond the immediate transition period, as ANC women activists were elected to parliament in subsequent post-conflict elections. Looking back, Ginwala concluded that ANC women's successes "did not happen out of nothing ... it is a process of which the MPs have been a part" (Geisler 2000, 607). As Ginwala suggests, women's successes were borne of a long struggle to which ANC

---

[1] David Kenvyn. "Frene Ginwa: Lawyer, Freedom Fighter, Political Leader, Stateswoman (1932–2023)." Action for Southern Africa, March 3, 2023. https://actsa.org/frene-ginwala-lawyer-freedom-fighter-political-leader-stateswoman-1932-2023/; Shireen Hassim. "Frene Ginwala Remembered: Trailblazing Feminist and First Speaker of South Africa's Democratic Parliament." The Conversation, January 13, 2023. https://theconversation.com/frene-ginwala-remembered-trailblazing-feminist-and-first-speaker-of-south-africas-democratic-parliament-197851.

women were committed both during and after the fight against apartheid. ANC female MPs' wartime roles positioned them to continue advocating for their political goals in elected office. In fact, many of the women running on the ANC ticket were deeply embedded in the organization's earlier fight against apartheid (Geisler 2000). This embeddedness offered them the clout and influence with which to pursue their policy goals.

ANC women's success in pushing post-conflict policy is illuminating not only because they were able to leverage their wartime roles into postwar gains, but also because it demonstrates that long-term gains for women demand sustained post-conflict activism, some of which takes place within government institutions and includes female militants.

Sudan's 2005 comprehensive peace agreement further underscores the challenges militant women face when trying to introduce provisions that benefit women into peace agreements and the strategies they pursue to ensure the terms' implementation after conflicts end. Women buoyed the multi-decade rebellion staged by the Sudan People's Liberation Movement (SPLM), even fighting on the frontlines alongside men. Despite their centrality to the movement, few women were initially included in the peace process, and they struggled to have their demands heard. The peace agreement included gender-inclusive peace terms, but they were watered down and vague. For example, the SPLM's women members and other female activists advocated for the inclusion of a 25% gender quota, but the final agreement only included a provision establishing that men and women would have equal social and political rights without detailing measures by which those goals would be achieved. Disappointment with the terms written into the agreement led SPLM female cadres to use their residual wartime political influence to ensure women made greater post-conflict gains. Electoral politics became a vehicle by which these militant women built and then maintained post-conflict power; they used their roles as elected Members of Parliament (MPs) and cabinet members to continue pushing their demands after the peace process concluded. Importantly, after the first postwar election, women parliamentarians' and activists' successful mobilization led to the adoption of the 25% gender quota they were unable to achieve during negotiations (Tønnessen and al-Nagar 2013). Minister Anne Itto, a former SPLM combatant and peace delegate during the negotiation process, proffered that the implementation process was paramount to the actual provisions listed in the peace agreement, as an agreement that goes unimplemented is meaningless (Itto 2006). Thus, Itto and her SPLM colleagues made sure the window of opportunity for rebel women to usher in change did not close fully when the conflicts terminated. Instead, former female rebels used the implementation process as an additional opening to influence political and social outcomes for women. In this Element, we show that former rebel women seize these opportunities and do so with great effect.

Much of the scholarship on women in peace processes and postwar transitions shows that women's inclusion leads to better outcomes for women and peace broadly (Duque-Salazar et al. 2022; Ellerby 2016; Krause et al. 2018; Reid 2021; True and Riveros-Morales 2019). Yet, extant research focuses mainly on how women affect the adoption of gendered provisions within negotiated settlements, offering less insight into whether and how these promises are implemented. As the narratives from South Africa and Sudan suggest, however, the push for gender-inclusive policies – and the attendant effects of these advancements – does not conclude with the signing of a peace settlement. Rather, it involves a lengthy and often arduous fight to implement these policies, in which women play a key role. Without implementation, the gains these settlements' promise to women remain little more than "scraps of paper."

In this project, we consider women's roles in the implementation of gendered policies after war. We build on the rich literature on women's inclusion during peace processes to ask how women influence compliance with the gendered provisions included in peace agreements. Our research contributes to this body of work by shifting focus from asking when and why peace agreements contain gender-inclusive terms to examining the extent to which parties attempt to implement these terms written into agreements. In other words, we seek to better understand when the promises in agreements become realized. Further, we consider how the electoral process can provide opportunities for women who were members of former non-state armed groups like the ANC and SPLM to affect the implementation process after wars abate. We ask specifically how women's representation in *rebel parties* – violent armed groups that transition into political parties – can impact compliance with gender-inclusive peace agreement terms. Finally, we explore whether women legislators' wartime connections to rebel groups affect the realization of the policies laid out in gendered peace provisions.

We conceptualize gendered provisions as any peace agreement provisions that reference women, girls, gender, or gender-based/sexual violence (Bell et al. 2024). Data suggests 39% of peace agreements between 1990 and 2018 include such provisions (Olson Lounsbery et al. 2024). These terms have become even more prevalent since the passage of United Nations Security Council resolution (UNSC) 1325 (Olson Lounsbery et al. 2024), as nearly half of the agreements between 2000 and 2016 include at least one gender-inclusive agreement term (True and Riveros-Morales 2019). Sudan's 2011 Doha agreement stipulated, for example, that "in accordance with the UNSCR 1325 (2000), the Commission shall ensure that all forms of violence that specifically affect women and children are heard and redressed in a gender sensitive and competent manner."[2] Burundi's 2006 Dar-es-Salaam agreement proposed that the country's prospective "Truth and Reconciliation Commission shall ... reflect the broadest representation of the Burundi society in its political, social, ethnic, religious and gender aspects."[3] Colombia's 2016 Comprehensive Peace Agreement provides a much more detailed example in asserting the following: "taking account of the fact that women face greater social and institutional barriers in terms of political participation, as a result of deep-rooted discrimination and inequality, as well as structural conditions of exclusion and subordination, there will be significant challenges in guaranteeing their right to participation and facing up to and transforming these historical conditions will involve developing affirmative measures that will safeguard women's participation in the various areas of political and social representation."[4]

Using a novel dataset on the implementation of gender provisions in African peace agreements, we find evidence that women's national representation and the representation of ex-rebel women are associated with higher levels of implementation of gender peace provisions. We complement these findings with brief illustrative cases from Angola, Rwanda, and Colombia. We find support for our key argument in the African cases. We use our illustrative case of Colombia to explore how these findings may travel, but emphasize the need for further data collection to confirm that our argument generalizes to other regions.

Our novel research draws together two related, though frequently siloed, bodies of literature: that on women, peace, and security and that on rebel party transitions. Previous work on the role of women in peace processes emphasizes the importance of women gaining a seat at the negotiating table and the adoption of gendered peace provisions, but fails to consider whether women's continued presence and pressure impact when such provisions come to life. At the same time, the research on rebel party politics demonstrates the importance of these political organizations and their memberships in supporting or threatening postwar peace but focuses more on conflict relapse and peace durability than on how these organizations promote compliance with specific agreement terms or whether group-level characteristics such as gender diversity impact the implementation process. While newer work has begun to consider women's

---

[2] "Doha Document for Peace in Darfur (DDPD)." www.peaceagreements.org/media/documents/ag853_5630ed637d2b6.pdf.

[3] Dar es Salaam Agreement to Principles toward Lasting Peace, Security and Stability in Burundi. www.peaceagreements.org/media/documents/ag702_5631fd316392f.pdf.

[4] "Final Agreement to End the Armed Conflict and Build a Stable and Lasting Peace." www.peaceagreements.org/media/documents/ag1845_593e97bdd6f32.pdf.

representation in rebel parties, it has focused mainly on explaining patterns of their descriptive representation rather than assessing their substantive impact. In the sections that follow, we discuss these bodies of literature in greater depth, highlighting how we build on previous work to advance our understanding of women's roles in the implementation processes. We then offer an overview of our theoretical argument and findings. We conclude with a summary of the sections of this Element.

1.1 Women's Inclusion, Gender Policies, and Peace Transitions

Though war has detrimental and often uneven impacts on the livelihoods and security of women, it can also usher in a "window of opportunity," in which women find avenues to carve out space for themselves in political, social, and economic spheres of life that would have been unthinkable prior to the war. War is associated with short and medium-term gains in women's empowerment (Webster et al. 2019). Women's political representation also often rises after wars, in part due to institutional changes like the adoption of gender quotas and pressure from international and domestic women activists (Tripp 2015). Women's rights after wars also increase as new constitutions are drafted and implemented (Tripp 2016). Moreover, gains for women offer broad benefits to a state's postwar peace, security, and stability, as many scholars find that higher levels of women's political representation are associated with a lower likelihood of conflict relapse and longer peace duration after war (Demeritt et al. 2014; Shair-Rosenfield and Wood 2017). These findings accord with the research demonstrating negative relationships between women's participation in politics, on one hand, and the likelihood of military crises (Caprioli 2000, 2005), human rights abuses (Melander 2005b), and conflict severity (Melander 2005a) on the other.

Women's inclusion in peace processes can also lead to distinctive and consequential outcomes. First, peace negotiations that include women are likelier to end in signed agreements, and resulting agreements are more readily implemented (O'Reilly et al. 2015). Women's participation is also correlated with a longer duration of post-conflict peace (Krause et al. 2018). Women's participation in the formal peace process creates positive externalities for women, as gendered peace provisions are likelier to be adopted when women serve in peace delegations (Anderson 2015; Ellerby 2016; True and Riveros-Morales 2019), especially in more central roles (Good 2024). Finally, peace agreements that include gendered provisions are associated with higher levels of women's rights after wars (Reid 2021), as well as increased civil liberties and political representation (Bakken and Buhaug 2020).

Scholars have offered many explanations for how women produce such positive outcomes. In general, the successful adoption of gender provisions in agreements is the result of significant, sustained advocacy by women activists, including those with a formal seat at the table and those without. First, women's inclusion in the peace process can broaden the perspectives that are represented and diversify the interests of those negotiating – ensuring the process better embodies the interests of society (Anderlini 2000; Anderson 2015; Ellerby 2016; Paffenholz et al. 2016). Moreover, female negotiators draw attention to women's issues and advocate for provisions that begin to address these concerns. Second, women in peace processes are often effective at building influential cross-cutting coalitions that reach across the aisle to women in other delegations and foster ties with women in civil society groups (Krause et al. 2018; O'Reilly et al. 2015; Paffenholz et al. 2016). These broad, diverse alliances increase the chance that the warring sides are able to find common ground and enable negotiating parties to generate settlements that are more reflective of society at large (Krause et al. 2018). These processes result in more expeditious and equitable peace settlements (Tamaru and O'Reilly 2018).

For example, when the Colombian government first sat down at the negotiating table with the Revolutionary Armed Forces of Colombia-People's Army (FARC-EP) in 2012, there was only one woman included in the FARC-EP delegation, and the government delegation had no women representatives (Céspedes-Báez and Ruiz 2018). This sparked outrage among women's groups, including civil society leaders, FARC-EP women guerrillas, and international activists, who all put mounting pressure on the delegations to put forth a more inclusive slate. This pressure led the Colombian process to become the most gender-inclusive peace process to date (Bouvier 2016). A key pressure point was the coalition between militant and nonmilitant women. Similarly, in Guatemala, Luz Mendez, a former United National Revolutionary Unity (URNG) guerrilla, was one of just two women appointed to the negotiation team. However, she was forceful in promoting women's rights during the peace process and was aided by a coalition that included women's civil society organizations (Krause et al. 2018). This alliance ensured that the resultant provisions were representative of a broad array of women's interests (Méndez 2005).

Though the potential payoffs of women's inclusion are high, the path to inclusion is still littered with hindrances. Women are largely underrepresented in these processes. Between 1992 and 2019, women accounted for only 13% of mediators, 6% of signatories, and 6% of negotiators in peace processes.[5] Even

---

[5] Council on Foreign Relations. "Women's Participation in Peace Processes." Accessed February 14, 2025. www.cfr.org/womens-participation-in-peace-processes/explore-the-data.

when women occupy one of the rare seats at the table, gendered hierarchies hinder their ability to contribute equally (Anderson and Golan 2023). Women's expertise is often assumed to be limited to "women's issues," excluding them from other critical discussions (Aharoni 2011; Ellerby 2013). Furthermore, even with regard to the adoption of gendered provisions, negotiating actors often push back against the inclusion of these provisions despite significant international support and pressure for their inclusion (Hirblinger et al. 2019; Itto 2006; Paffenholz et al. 2016).

Moreover, recent scholarship cements the idea that it matters *which* women are included in peace processes. In particular, new studies show that the specific women at the table can influence the possibilities for peace and the outcomes of conciliation. Brannon and Best (2022), for example, demonstrate that delegations' selection criteria can affect the quality of women's contributions, as women selected for their reliability and loyalty may be more likely to uphold the status quo and toe the party line. Likewise, Paffenholz et al. (2016) suggest that in the Philippines, the selection of female delegates, who were mainly wives and family members of rebel leaders, stunted coalition building among women delegates, as the women affiliated with the rebels were unwilling to cross the party line. Research has also begun to show that women's representation within militant groups can influence the conflict resolution process. Brannon et al. (2024) for example, show that gender-diverse rebel groups are more likely to participate in peace talks with the state, and this can be attributed, in part, to the propensity for armed groups that recruit women to make peace overtures more frequently. At the same time, women's participation in rebel groups can affect which gendered policies are advanced in peace settlements. Since rebel women have distinct interests from nonmilitant women, their inclusion increases the chances that gendered provisions relevant to their interests as combatants and women from marginalized backgrounds are adopted (Thomas 2023).

While the scholarship on gender and peace processes has offered a rich understanding of the causes, consequences, and complications of women's roles in peace processes, little is known about the implementation of these terms post-conflict. Gender peace provisions can fall by the wayside after wars end, and outside pressure on and attention to these issues dissipates. Moreover, many gendered provisions require longer time horizons and sustained attention for them to be implemented successfully since they often require that underlying gender relations are restructured and inequalities are redressed (Joshi et al. 2020). One of the few inquiries into this question suggests women's mobilization – mainly through civil society organizations – can encourage the implementation of gender-inclusive stipulations but only where governments are willing to prioritize gender issues (Duque-Salazar et al. 2022). Extant research has overlooked the key question of when and why a state might come to view gender issues as priorities and has not examined the full range of women's coalitions that could be mobilized to facilitate this process. Our research fills this lacuna, offering deeper insight into women's contributions to postwar peace and gender politics.

1.2 The Implementation of Peace Agreements

While a body of research has examined the dynamics and outcomes of negotiated settlements or peace processes, there has been less scholarly attention on the implementation of such agreements. Although conflict negotiations represent an important step in securing peace, the negotiation stage does not represent a "definitive endpoint" of conflict (Mockinlay et al. 2005, 4). Likewise, though monumental, the signing of peace agreements marks only the beginning of peacebuilding efforts. The post-agreement period can be rife with uncertainty about former warring parties' commitments to uphold their side of the bargain. Thus, the efficacy of an agreement and the peace it creates depends on whether its provisions are implemented (Joshi and Wallensteen 2018; Mockinlay et al. 2005; Stedman 2001). Joshi and Quinn (2017) argue that the implementation of agreements is even more critical than the negotiation process because it normalizes relationships between formerly hostile groups, solves credible commitment and information problems, and perhaps most importantly, addresses the root causes of the civil conflict. The degree to which agreements are implemented thus affects post-conflict peace duration and decreases the chances of future conflict eruption or reoccurrence (Joshi and Quinn 2016, 2017; Joshi and Wallensteen 2018; Stedman 2001).

Former rebels' buy-in is foundational to the implementation of these agreements, as they can act as spoilers to these processes or as bulwarks against backsliding. Former rebel groups' transformation into political parties (rebel parties), a provision frequently written into contemporary negotiated agreements (Matanock 2017, 2018), can play a sizable role in shaping the direction of the implementation process. Former rebel parties' commitments to the use of institutionalized and peaceful means to drive policy, and their willingness to make political compromises, can help ensure that the transition from war to postwar politics is peaceful (Lyons 2016a). Moreover, when rebel parties gain political power and influence through the electoral process, their cooperation becomes necessary to advance the implementation process (Mockinlay et al. 2005). Where they hold significant power, rebel parties can shape which provisions are implemented and how.

Scholars have studied how rebel party behavior influences the stability of the implementation period. Studies have considered how vulnerability and competition among former belligerents impacts perceived costs and benefits of reigniting war (Bekoe 2003, 2005), how guaranteed spoils in the form of government positions improve implementation and peace duration (Hartzell and Hoddie 2003; Jarstad and Nilsson 2008; Joshi et al. 2017a), and how wartime party structures and intra-elite competition among former rebels parties influence rebels' capacity to successfully adapt to new, institutionalized political rules of the game (Ishiyama and Batta 2011; Ishiyama and Widmeier 2020; Lyons 2016b; Manning 2004, 2007). Much of this work suggests implementation is affected by the iterative nature of inter- and intra-party relationships. Among all political parties in government, including rebel parties, priorities are informed by actors' needs to differentiate themselves from other parties through policy spoils for supporters, and the degree to which they want to appear willing to cooperate with their opposition (Joshi et al. 2017a; Joshi and Quinn 2017). Intra-party conflict can also shape priorities, particularly in newly formed rebel parties. Studies suggest that rebel party leaders must have buy-in from elites and majority coalitions for agreements to succeed (Bekoe 2003, 2005; Lyons 2016b; Mockinlay et al. 2005). Former combatants, who maintain significant sway over their former rebel parties after wars end, are also influential in this process (Sindre 2016a, 2016b).

Broadly, this work suggests rebel party politics can have a significant influence on the uptake of an implementation process. Namely, compliance with a peace agreement will be determined by the interests of those who hold power and those who support the relevant powerbrokers. Following this logic, we contend that when women are among those who hold power, gendered peace agreement provisions are more likely to be translated into post-conflict law and practice. To date, existing work has not considered the role of gender – whether that is the influence of women in rebel parties or how rebel parties prioritize gender-inclusive provisions – in influencing how organizations approach fulfilling their obligations to the peace process. This oversight is glaring given the many ways women affect rebel organizational dynamics and the peace process more specifically.

1.3 Theoretical Argument

In this Element, we argue that women drive the implementation of gendered peace provisions after wars. Though we consider the effect of women's national representation, we focus primarily on women who are elected representatives in rebel parties, who can use their positions to encourage the implementation of gendered peace provisions. We expect, however, that women representatives' ability to impact the implementation process is conditioned by their positionality within postwar political power structures. It is important to focus on the role of women within former rebel parties since former belligerents – particularly those that attain post-conflict political power – can wield significant influence over the state's implementation priorities after war. Women's roles within these parties offer them access and leverage to shape the implementation of agreements, specifically gendered provisions. Moreover, rebel women's wartime networks and experiences uniquely position them to hold their former organizations accountable for the commitments they made during peace negotiations.

We test three implications of this broad argument. First, we explore whether women's national level of political representation is associated with higher levels of implementation of gendered peace provisions. This builds on research that suggests women's inclusion in peace processes generally leads to better outcomes with regard to gendered provisions and peace duration. Second, we examine whether rebel parties with a higher percentage of women party members are likelier to push for the implementation of gender peace provisions, following research suggesting the proportion of women within wartime rebel movements correlates with the inclusion of gendered agreement terms. Third, we consider differences among women representatives in rebel parties, arguing that not all women within these parties have an equal impact on peace agreement implementation. Although any women within a post-rebel party might impact the implementation of gender-inclusive terms, we argue that the recruitment of a greater number of women who served in the rebel group during the war will amplify women's influence over implementation because rebel women will maintain closer network ties to rebel elites and are more likely to have been involved in the process of negotiating gendered stipulations. By examining these three forms of women's representation, we seek to understand *which* women impact the implementation of gendered peace provisions as well as how women's positions within wartime networks influence postwar gender politics.

Throughout our argument, we highlight the distinct role of former rebel women represented in rebel parties. We argue that women's presence in key positions of power within post-conflict governments can increase the chance of implementation. Our argument is probabilistic, not determinative, however. We do not expect women rebel party legislators to always affect implementation. We also do not believe women's participation in rebellion is sufficient to ensure gender provisions are implemented. Instead, we argue that women's appointment to government roles through rebel parties is crucial, though we also accept that there are limits to what they can accomplish.

Moreover, we do not expect that former rebel women alone drive implementation. We hypothesize that women legislators writ large can also positively affect implementation, though we argue rebel women can act as critical agents in these environments.[6] We proffer that former rebel women will be crucial nodes in legislative networks, influencing rebel party politics through their wartime ties and building coalitions with other women legislators. Though there may be a small number of ex-rebel women elected, research on women and politics has demonstrated that a small minority of actors within legislatures can still have a significant effect on outcomes (Bratton 2005; Crowley 2011). Thus, we expect that even if rebel women represent a minority of seats in the legislature, they may still have an important and unique effect on implementation.

1.4 Overview

Our Element is organized as follows: In the next section, we ground our study in previous research on former wartime belligerents, commitment problems, and powersharing. We present our theoretical argument in Section 3. In Section 4, we offer our research design and present our novel dataset on the implementation of gender peace agreement provisions. Section 5 offers an empirical analysis of our core arguments, which proposes that women's representation in rebel parties will be associated with greater implementation of gender-inclusive peace provisions. We first test the relationship between women's national representation and implementation, finding evidence that women's political representation in national parliaments fosters implementation. We then consider the role of women representatives within rebel parties, finding mixed results regarding their impact on implementation. Our final test most directly tests our argument by considering the effect of female representatives of rebel parties that were former combatants, finding robust evidence that higher levels of female ex-rebel representation in rebel parties is associated with higher rates of implementation. We bolster these statistical tests with qualitative evidence from Angola, Rwanda, and Colombia.

In Section 6, we conclude by highlighting our contributions to several bodies of literature, including gender and peace processes, rebel party politics, and women's roles in peace transitions. We discuss the real-world implications of our findings, especially how our findings call for revisions to the current

---

[6] We adopt Childs and Krook's (2009) definition of critical actors as "those who who act individually or collectively to bring about women-friendly policy change," (127).

iteration of the Women, Peace, and Security agenda. We conclude with a discussion of important questions that emerge from our theory and findings.

2 Former Rebel Parties and the Implementation of Peace

Although peace agreements are not merely "scraps of paper" (Fortna 2003), reaching a deal does not guarantee peace or ensure that the issues underlying a conflict are resolved. Resolving these issues, however, is key to sustainable peace (Werner 1999). While treaties are often carefully designed to address belligerents' grievances, there are often substantial barriers to their full implementation. Peace processes can be impeded by warring parties' lack of will and inability to follow through with their commitments. Issues that might be deemed ancillary are especially likely to be neglected during this implementation phase. Sidelining these "secondary" issues is especially likely to impact the implementation of gender-inclusive peace terms since even the rebel groups that push for women's interests often cast gender issues as subordinate to the primary conflict issues. Even while promoting women's inclusion, militant organizations, such as the Mozambique Liberation Front (FRELIMO), Communist Party of Nepal-Maoist (CPN-M), and the ANC have conceptualized women's issues as ancillary and secondary to the main lines of conflict (Brechenmacher and Hubbard 2020; Katto 2014; Pavarti 2005). When the need to prioritize certain provisions arises, belligerents may be especially unfaithful to gender-inclusive terms.

Given the tendency for implementing parties to prioritize some provisions over others, the enactment of gender-inclusive peace agreement terms may be observed only under certain conditions. To affect implementation, rebel parties first need to have access to the reins of power. We conceptualize access to power as the ability to participate in the legislature as an official political party. Although there are other mechanisms of rebel-state powersharing, we argue that the ability to compete in elections provides rebels with the means and opportunity to contest power over the long term. While other types of power-sharing institutions include temporary provisions that enable rebels to share power during a transitional administration, the ability to take part in elections in the future allows rebels to impact implementation after these temporary institutions are replaced.

Since we are particularly interested in the enactment of gender-inclusive peace terms, we believe women within these former rebel parties will play a key role. First, we suggest that the implementation of gender peace provisions will be higher when women's national representation is higher. This is consistent with extant research that suggests women have played an important role in the negotiation and adoption of gendered peace terms. Second, we assert that the implementation of these provisions will be more likely when women make up a greater share of rebel party legislators. We consider how women within rebel parties may be able to shift priorities and the behavior of former belligerents. Third, we argue that women representatives in rebel parties who were wartime members will have a particularly potent effect on implementation outcomes because they are both able to derive clout from their affiliations with former rebel groups and draw on their wartime (and postwar) coalitions and networks to push for gendered policies. We build this argument, starting with how bargaining problems, powersharing, and resource constraints cause negotiating parties to prioritize some provisions over others and then explaining why rebel-party transitions and women's representation will help overcome these issues.

2.1 Bargaining Dynamics, Powersharing, and Implementing Peace Agreements

Warring parties often sign peace agreements under immense pressure to end bloodshed, which affects the implementation of post-conflict peace agreements. Belligerents are often faced with the choice to either continue conflict or settle for a subpar bargain. When parties opt for imperfect settlements, agreements may end up including terms that at least one side is displeased with and has little incentive to comply with after violence abates. Since negotiations and concessions are often acceded to when pressure and pain are at their height (Pechenkina and Thomas 2020; Thomas 2014; Zartman 2005), a signed agreement does not necessarily ensure warring parties will uphold their commitments when circumstances change.

Commitment problems often affect whether parties honor the terms in agreements. Belligerents' interests in terms of peace can change with expectations about their future strength. Time inconsistency problems, which occur when governments or rebels believe their military capabilities will improve with time, can prevent the implementation of the agreed-upon terms, as parties have incentives to accept peace even if they plan to renege on their promises later (Werner 1999). The possibility of these changing interests is particularly concerning for rebels, who are often expected to demobilize before the government makes any headway on upholding their end of the bargain (Fortna 2003; Johnson 2021; Walter 2002). The essence of the commitment problem known to impair civil war settlement and engender conflict recurrence is that parties sign deals that are ultimately unenforceable (Walter 1997, 2002, 2009).

As Stedman (2001, 1) notes, periods directly following the signing of a civil war peace agreement are "fraught with risk, uncertainty, and vulnerability for the warring parties and civilians caught in between." Those seeking to comply with the agreement can be waylaid by spoilers, which may emerge from both within and outside of the peace process (Stedman 1997). Inside spoilers, which can include both governments and rebels, may not always rely on violence; they may sabotage peace by simply failing to implement key parts of an agreement. Scholars argue, however, that settlements can be designed with features to minimize these risks (Mattes and Savun 2009); security guarantees and power-sharing, for instance, are believed to attenuate commitment problems and lead to more durable peace (Beardsley 2008; Walter 1997, 2009).

Powersharing terms appear in half of all comprehensive peace settlements (Joshi and Quinn 2015). Previous research finds that when former belligerents share power in post-conflict environments, peace accords are likelier to be implemented and peace is more enduring (Hartzell and Hoddie 2003; Mattes and Savun 2009). According to Hartzell and Hoddie (2003, 320), power-sharing institutions refer to "rules that, in addition to defining how decisions will be made by groups within the polity, allocate decision-making rights, including access to state resources, among collectivities competing for power." Referring to ethnic powersharing in particular, Roeder and Rothchild (2005, 31) argue that powersharing institutions aim "to reassure minorities that their interests will be taken into account by guaranteeing the participation of representatives of all the main ethnic groups in the making of governmental decisions." To have this mollifying effect, representatives need to have access to actual power, which means tokenism – or the accommodation of only a couple of a group's representatives – is insufficient to provide such assurances (Roeder and Rothchild 2005).

Among the four types of powersharing institutions (i.e., political, economic, military, territorial), scholars have homed in on political powersharing – including electoral proportional representation – as particularly stabilizing (Mattes and Savun 2009; Walter 2002).[7] Mukherjee (2006, 411) argues that "providing political representation to minorities and leaders of insurgent groups increases their stakes in the political process and reduces their incentives to fight against the state." Political powersharing can also limit belligerents' ability to renege on bargains (Mattes and Savun 2009), which increases the chance that agreements are implemented and peace prevails. Powersharing institutions also help manage belligerents' mistrust and help parties alter their expectations and perceptions of their opponents (Joshi et al. 2017; Joshi and Quinn 2015).

---

[7] Mukherjee (2006) suggests powersharing arrangements are most stabilizing when they are offered in the context of a decisive victory.

Scholars also argue that the creation of transitional institutions and rebel-to-party transitions, which transform and demilitarize politics, can prove vital for durable peace (Lyons 2015; Spears 2000). Such rebel party transitions are most prevalent in Africa (Manning et al. 2024). Even though electoral contests may be seen as more advantageous to states (Johnson 2021), electoral participation provisions offer a path for rebels to contend in elections and can produce more stable and longer-lasting peace, as these terms encourage parties to uphold their ends of compromise agreements (Matanock 2017).

Rebels' successful integration into postwar governments can facilitate continued bargaining that can accommodate changing interests. Since formal bargaining continues in the post-accord period (Bekoe 2003), a time marked by mutual vulnerability and suspicion (Joshi et al. 2017), sharing power can create opportunities for former belligerents to work together to make decisions if wartime negotiations prove insufficient in the post-conflict environment (Lyons 2015). Difficulties and disagreements inevitably arise during the implementation process, but when parties can address issues in real time, disagreements are less likely to derail peace (Hartzell and Hoddie 2003). Moreover, a commitment to implementation can be a costly signal of a belligerent's dedication to peace (Hoddie and Hartzell 2005).

The joint work of implementing agreements can solve common bargaining issues – including information and commitment problems, help address the root causes of conflict, and normalize political relationships between former warring parties (Joshi and Quinn 2015). Powersharing helps ensure compliance with an agreement because it enables rebel groups to act as a check on the state, which might otherwise attempt to evade implementation (Joshi et al. 2017). Together, powersharing arrangements and verification provisions increase the likelihood of an agreement's implementation (Joshi et al. 2017). Offering rebels a stake in the implementation process can increase their ownership over and buy-in to the implementation of the peace process (Molloy and Bell 2019). In some cases, the implementation process can be a task delegated specifically to coalition governments, which include former rebels (Molloy and Bell 2019).

According to Joshi and Quinn (2015, 873), the day-to-day process of implementation can enable belligerents to "work together to represent their constituencies and gain recognition for themselves in the process." While representing their supporters, rebels in post-conflict governments can also advance their own political interests peacefully (Joshi and Mason 2011). Rebels use negotiated settlements to alter the political status quo, renegotiate the distribution of power (Joshi and Quinn 2015), and expand the size of the winning coalition (Joshi and Mason 2011). The latter can increase the value of providing public goods and reduce the risk of returning to conflict. Indeed, many agreements include terms that cater to a broad civilian constituency, including provisions for the reduction of poverty, discrimination, and repression (Joshi and Quinn 2015).

However, even when belligerents have the will to implement and are able to overcome bargaining obstacles, they may lack the ability to fully comply with the agreements they sign under duress. Low state capacity, in particular, can threaten implementation even when states want to follow through (DeRouen et al. 2010). Implementation needs willingness but also resources for parties to be able to stick to the bargains (Karreth et al. 2019). Yet, states emerging from long and costly civil wars often lack the resources to effectively implement the terms of the agreements (Stedman et al. 2002). Since peace agreements often contain a wide range of provisions that need to be implemented to meet the full set of agreement terms (Stedman et al. 2002), states facing a resource shortfall may find full compliance with an agreement particularly challenging. Resource constraints can lead states to prioritize some terms over others. Terms that do not address the state's immediate concerns may be implemented later than others or not at all. Stedman et al. (2002, 3) suggest the decision for states to follow through with their commitments in civil war rests on their willingness to "invest blood and treasure" and their belief that a peace settlement will advance the state's security interests. However, how they prioritize these terms after the war will vary.

2.2 Variation in Implementation by Provision Type

The combination of bargaining, powersharing, and resource challenges can lead to differences in how specific provisions are implemented. Both the threat of commitment problems derailing peace and the menace of resource constraints have led some scholars to advocate for sequencing the implementation of peace agreement terms (Joshi et al. 2017). This simply calls for some types of provisions to be prioritized over others. For durable peace, scholars argue that belligerents should address commitment problems before they introduce other political changes, including holding post-conflict elections (Joshi et al. 2017). Some research suggests post-conflict stability requires states to prioritize demobilization, disarmament, and reintegration and the demilitarization of politics (Spears 2000; Stedman et al. 2002). Judicial reforms and improvements to human rights capacity are also important ways to ensure that peace sticks and conflicts do not recur (Spears 2000; Stedman et al. 2002). Moreover, scholars suggest that belligerents may choose to deviate from agreements as written to address changing interests and updated calculations (Lyons 2015). These deviations become more likely as attention shifts away from third-party preferences and toward localization of the peace process. Thus, states may prioritize peace agreement terms that reflect these imperatives over other terms that are in agreements, including those that address women's interests and needs.

Compliance with the terms of peace agreements is also more difficult when the terms constitute greater deviations from the status quo (Ozcelik 2020). Thus, provisions focusing on women or gender are less likely to be implemented when ideas of gender inclusion and equality deviate substantially from existing law and practice and when there is less organic domestic interest and support for such provisions. In other words, the implementation of gender-inclusive provisions may be less likely when belligerents are pressured into including these terms, possibly by third parties or even domestic actors, than when those issues are inherently of interest to one or both sides. Stedman et al. (2002) argue that "peace agreements are quintessential coalition-based documents that stem in part from demands of constituencies beyond the warring parties themselves." Taking these preferences into account can lead to the inclusion of terms that cater specifically to third parties but do not reflect the interests of conflict actors. Downs and Stedman (2002) suggest that due to the advocacy of human rights NGOs, peace processes after the 1990s may have been overly ambitious in their inclusion of provisions aimed at improving women's rights, in addition to other key human rights concerns, such as child soldiering and de-mining. Similarly, Stedman et al. (2002) suggest the integration of such terms may hinder implementation. Given limited resources and short time horizons, implementing parties often lack the motivation or ability to address these goals (Downs and Stedman 2002). So, despite their inclusion in an agreement, supplemental provisions may be given short shrift during implementation.

Post-agreement, when implementing parties contend with resource constraints and the need to address commitment problems adequately, parties may decide to deprioritize the provisions that were included to placate the disparate coalitions and factions that emerged during the peace process – including those that improve women's lives – in lieu of security-related provisions. We contend, however, that decisions to deprioritize gender-inclusive peace terms are short-sighted given the groundswell of evidence that boosting women's rights, welfare, political participation, and economic empowerment can be a boon to peace durability and post-conflict stability (Krause et al. 2018; O'Reilly et al. 2015; Tamaru and O'Reilly 2018). These findings provide evidence that gender-inclusive peace terms *are* security-related provisions. However, parties in conflict rarely see it this way. Given that an immediate focus on demobilizing and integrating former belligerents as a security guarantee is often prioritized, even well-meaning actors are unlikely to rush to implement terms that they view as peripheral or ancillary to the goal of immediate peace. Thus, we can expect that, on average, gender-inclusive provisions will not be among the first terms implemented in most peace processes.

Echavarría Álvarez et al. (2022) find that fewer gender-conscious provisions have been implemented than what they term "general" provisions. Joshi et al. (2020) find that despite an unprecedented number of gender-specific stipulations included in Colombia's comprehensive peace agreement, only 9% of these provisions were fully implemented three years after the accord was signed, compared to 25% of non-gender-specific terms. Whereas 33% of non-gender-specific terms were uninitiated after three years, more than 47% of Colombia's gendered peace terms had not yet begun by 2019. Only 7% of the agreements inked during the years 2000–2016 included any specific guidelines for implementing the gender-inclusive provisions incorporated into agreements (UN Women 2018, 33), which offers additional insight into the poor track record for the implementation of gender-inclusive peace terms. These statistics suggest a significant difference in how gender-inclusive provisions are approached compared to non-gender-inclusive terms.

Whether and how rebels view implementing gender provisions remains underexplored. In general, we expect that agreement terms – especially those rebels advocate for – are more likely to be prioritized during the implementation phase when rebel group affiliates meaningfully participate in the government. We argue this can happen through several channels, but we focus on institutions where rebels take part in the administration of the state. We pay particular attention to cases where rebels gain access to power through post-conflict elections for two primary reasons. First, the election of rebel parties to legislatures fits broadly within the concept of post-conflict powersharing. Second, when rebels are elected, they have a popular mandate and may have more public support for the policies they advocate for. This public support may put greater pressure on the state and other powerbrokers to remain faithful in the implementation process. It can also give rebels political cover for demanding the implementation of certain provisions. These avenues ensure that rebels have influence over which provisions are implemented and how.

Further, we expect that rebels' motivation to implement provisions may vary by provision type. Rebels are not only interested in implementation to gain the personal benefits they are allotted in peace agreements, but they also push for implementation to placate their civilian audiences, who typically prefer peace over continued war (Prorok and Cil 2022). Studies suggest former rebel parties become more inclusive and more moderate after they transition because of their need to woo voters and broaden their support bases (Storm 2020). Maintaining public support becomes even more important as rebels eye future electoral competitions. Moreover, Bramble and Paffenholz (2020, 37) remind us that public support for peace agreements is essential, as elite-focused processes may still fail on popular referendum, as they did in both Guatemala and Colombia. Additionally, scholars have argued that where civilians doubt the trustworthiness of government promises of implementation, rebel groups can act as brokers of legitimacy for the state to ensure the viability of the peace process from which they stand to benefit (Breslawski 2023; Dyrstad et al. 2021). Thus, given both rebels' electoral incentives and their interest in maintaining the legitimacy of the peace process, a rebel organization can use the implementation of a peace accord to appeal to its civilian supporters.

We argue that women representatives in former rebel parties can play an important role in gaining civilian buy-in for the peace process writ large, as women have been found to increase acceptance of peace deals among conflict-affected populations (O'Reilly et al. 2015). At the same time, we also expect women's inclusion in rebel parties to impact that organization's willingness to implement gender-inclusive peace terms. Indeed, in Sub-Saharan Africa, transitional powersharing arrangements where rebel groups have participated in the government have been associated with improvements in women's empowerment and equal access to power more broadly (Johnson 2023). We unpack this to understand how women's representation may be creating such an effect. In the following sections, we discuss research on when and how gendered provisions are implemented and then consider how women's inclusion in legislatures impacts implementation, including women's national representation, women's representation in rebel parties, and specifically the inclusion of female ex-rebels in rebel parties.

3 The Implementation of Gender-Inclusive Provisions

While gender-inclusive peace agreement provisions tend to see lower levels of implementation on average (Echavarría Álvarez et al. 2022; Joshi et al. 2020), some conflicts do see the implementation of these provisions. Not only is there variation in warring parties' initial willingness to incorporate gender-inclusive peace terms in agreements (Anderson 2015; Krause et al. 2018; Thomas 2023), but as discussed, parties also vary in their willingness to implement these terms after wars end. We argue that the composition of the potential implementing contingent influences whether gender-inclusive provisions are given attention during peacetime. We believe women will be able to have greater influence over the implementation process when they are among the political insiders or powerbrokers.

When women participate in post-conflict governments, especially under the aegis of former rebel parties, advocacy for gendered provisions will not fall only to women from the incumbent government or third-party groups but can be taken up by those affiliated with former rebels and their coalitions. Expanding the government in this way ensures that a broader set of women have input in the implementation process, which should increase the chance that gender-inclusive provisions are implemented. Moreover, Joshi and Quinn (2015, 874) assert that in a viable implementation process, "outside groups generally lose support to political leaders now on the inside who are seen as exercising more power in the current political arrangement." Since women rebel party representatives constitute part of the primary warring faction and a core component of the current political constellation, their preferences and advocacy will be harder to sideline than the preferences and interests of third parties (e.g., civil society). This should benefit the implementation of gender-inclusive provisions.

We present a three-fold argument that specifies conditions under which gendered peace provisions are most likely to be implemented. First, women's national representation will influence the implementation of gendered peace provisions. Second, women's representation in rebel parties will improve the overall implementation of gendered peace agreements. Third, we argue that women representatives who served in the rebel group during the war will be even more effective at promoting implementation. Throughout these arguments, we focus on how these factors help solve the primary issues that affect implementation: commitment problems and resource allocations in the face of constraints. We discuss these ideas in turn.

3.1 Women's National Representation

Domestic actors have been responsible for ushering in unprecedented changes in women's rights after civil conflicts across the globe, but especially in Africa (Tripp 2016). Peace agreements create windows of opportunity for local women to push for substantial changes in gender regimes after war (Tripp 2015, 2016). Women's pressure and advocacy during the negotiation process have been instrumental in securing provisions that advance women's rights in peace agreements (Ellerby 2013; Krause et al. 2018; Reid 2021; True and Riveros-Morales 2019). African women activists have paved the way for significant changes in the post-agreement period as well. Rwandan women, for example, lobbied to be included in the post-conflict political environment after the country's civil war and genocide (Hogg 2009; Mageza-Barthel 2016; Powley 2003). Largely owing to their participation in drafting the state's post-conflict constitution and voting guidelines, Rwandan women were able to cement several consequential political changes, including a legislative quota and the establishment of a ministry of women's affairs.[8] Notably, the country instituted a quota mandating that 30% of the seats in their lower and upper parliament chambers would be set aside for women. The first post-conflict election in 2003 far surpassed this goal, with nearly 49% of the lower house being comprised of women (Devlin and Elgie 2008; Powley 2003). Although the series of agreements that were signed in 1992 and 1993 between the Republic of Rwanda and the Revolutionary Patriotic Front were not particularly notable for their gender inclusiveness, women's leadership in the post-conflict government led directly to the implementation of the gendered terms written into the various agreements. For instance, an October 1992 agreement called on the government to create the Ministry of Family Affairs and Promotion of the Status of Women.[9] In 1994, the RPF formed the new Ministry of Women and Family Protection with Aloisea Inyumba, former RPF finance commissioner, at the helm as minister (Hunt 2017). According to politician Fatuma Ndangiza, in the early days after the transition, "the ministry was spearheading women's advancement, gender equality, organizing from grassroots to the national level, empowering women in civil society" because there was not a preexisting blueprint (Hunt 2017, 110). Many of the ministry's early initiatives aimed at concentrating power into women's hands and promoting women's issues were eventually integrated into the constitution as permanent institutions.

The Rwandan case makes plain that an inclusive process is also important at the implementation stage. By contrast, experts suggest implementation is compromised when important groups, including women, are excluded (UN Women 2018). Evidence also demonstrates that accords are likelier to be implemented when women are at the table during peace processes (Krause et al. 2018; O'Reilly et al. 2015). Krause et al. (2018), for instance, find that when women are among an agreement's signatories, accords tend to include a greater range of terms, including those deemed vital for post-conflict stability (e.g., ceasefire commitment, disarmament, demobilization, reintegration, verification and monitoring, human rights, institutional reforms, development, women's rights). When women hold a salient formal role within the peace process as agreement signatories, these terms are generally also more likely to be implemented. Thus, women's representation in the peace process is central to the agreements' successful implementation.

---

[8] Gumisai Mutume. "Women Break into African Politics." Africa Renewal. April 2004. www.un.org/africarenewal/magazine/april-2004/women-break-african-politics.

[9] "The Protocol of Agreement between the Government of the Republic of Rwanda and the Rwandese Patriotic Front on Power-Sharing within the Framework of a Broad-based Transitional Government (Continuation of the Protocol of Agreement Signed on the October 30, 1992)." https://pax.peaceagreements.org/agreements/wgg/1343/.

We expect, then, that in post-conflict contexts, women legislators will also have a positive effect on the implementation of gender peace provisions. Moreover, when more women are elected at the national level, the average implementation rate of gender peace provisions will be higher.

3.2 Women's Representation in Rebel Parties

Though generally, we expect women legislators to positively affect implementation, the core of our argument is concerned with women represented in the former belligerent parties, whom we expect to have an even greater effect. To date, researchers and practitioners have focused largely on the important role civilian women play during peace processes. This emphasis is grounded in the idea that the civilian public is viewed as both a consequential stakeholder and a guarantor of peace (Braniff 2012). Indeed, scholars have demonstrated that women within civil society have left an indelible mark on shaping and implementing peace accords (Anderson 2015; Krause et al. 2018). Civil society can facilitate information gathering, which contributes to effective monitoring and verification of implementation progress (Ross 2017), particularly in inclusive processes (Verjee 2020). Women's participation in these monitoring teams has been crucial. For example, Barsa et al. (2016) argue that the women integrated into South Sudan's Monitoring and Verification Mission, including in community liaison positions, enhanced the mission's trust-building capabilities, ultimately improving the mission's ability to garner information from within conflict-affected communities. This increased transparency and information-gathering capability had a direct impact on the implementation of key parts of South Sudan's 2014 Cessation of Hostilities agreement, including obligations on the protection of civilians, as well as those regarding gender-based and sexual violence. Yet, when women lack a clear role during peace negotiations, it is often more difficult for them to find a concrete post-conflict role (Schädel and Dudouet 2020).

While the focus on the impact of and strategies to get more civil society women involved in peace processes is warranted, existing research has been myopic. It overlooks the potential opening that other women – particularly those aligned with rebel parties – may be able to use to get into the peace process. Our argument highlights the role women representatives from rebel parties play in the implementation process. In doing so, we do not aim to detract from the importance of women in civil society. Instead, we draw attention to another influential grouping of women that has largely been overlooked. While we argue that female representatives from former rebel parties have an advantage over other legislators in their push for the implementation of gender-inclusive peace terms, we also argue that women leaders, including those from civil society groups, constitute an important part of the implementation coalition that ultimately sees gender-inclusive provisions implemented.

Research suggests peace agreements are most likely to be implemented and peace is expected to be more durable when rebels share power in the wake of conflict termination. Rebels' participation in post-conflict elections has been found to reduce the likelihood of conflict recurrence and encourage democratization (Manning et al. 2024), while the exclusion of a major rebel party from a post-conflict government can increase the chance that peace fails and violence resumes (Marshall and Ishiyama 2018). Failing to include rebels meaningfully in post-conflict governments can exacerbate credible commitment problems and incentivize rebels to act as spoilers. Joo (2025) argues that rebels' participation in electoral politics can alleviate the dual commitment problem that exists after civil wars; powersharing arrangements can allay both governments' and rebels' fears. Participation in the country's inclusive institutions can enable former rebel groups to attain policy concessions, which can incentivize them to stick to peace. These incentives reduce the government's fears that rebels will turn back to war. Rebel parties' participation in state governance also allays rebels' fears that the government will renege on promises made during the peace negotiations. Governments that fail to uphold war-ending bargains risk not only renewed conflict but also electoral consequences of allowing peace to fail. Thus, governments that allow rebels to transition into rebel parties have strong incentives to accommodate rebel preferences and interests to forestall rebels' spoiling behavior.

In post-conflict settings, where states are keen to maintain peace and avoid conflict recurrence, the government has incentives to not only allow rebel groups to participate in a post-conflict government but assure rebels they have a true stake in the policy making process. Offering these veto players (and their representatives) a stake in the political process can reduce armed groups' incentives to return to conflict (Mukherjee 2006). States have similar incentives to carve out specific roles for former rebels in the implementation process to increase their buy-in to peace (Molloy and Bell 2019). As only veto players have a credible threat to "continue the war unilaterally, if one or more of these actors are not included in a peace process" (Cunningham 2013, 42), post-conflict governments do not have the same incentives to accommodate the preferences of non-veto player parties. Prioritizing rebel parties' preferences for the sake of post-conflict stability should diminish the influence of non-rebel parties relative to that of former rebel parties. We argue this dynamic will produce benefits for female legislators from rebel parties, which can be used to influence the implementation of gender peace terms.

We assert that gender-inclusive peace terms are more likely to be put into force when women are active in the implementation process, when they have access to the reins of power, and when gender-inclusive provisions are compatible with at least one of the primary warring parties' interests. This last point is especially crucial since implementers often prioritize the interests and needs of the primary belligerents over others' prerogatives in the wake of a conflict. For example, Verjee (2020, 8) reports that Sierra Leone's Commission for the Consolidation of Peace (CCP), one of its two monitoring and verification missions, was hamstrung by the preeminence of the warring factions within the institution. According to a former commissioner for the CCP, there were "no women in the commission, no disabled as a result of the war. People were thinking largely about warring factions. But we felt we [as civil society] had something to offer, and we had had a huge engagement in the peace process . . . We could have been very powerful, but the real power was with the [Revolutionary United Front] RUF and [Armed Forces Revolutionary Council (AFRC) leader Johnny] Koroma." Likewise, during the negotiation of Mali's 2015 Algiers Accord, under pressure to reach a timely deal, both the warring parties and third parties eschewed an inclusive process, which effectively shut out civil society and cut off a primary path for women's involvement (Schädel and Dudouet 2020). According to Kew and Wanis-St. John (2008, 18) "government and militant leaders, political party heads, warlords, and the usual cast of political elites driving the main forces in dispute – the ones with the guns – still get the lion's share of attention from international mediators," which has stymied the influence of local civil society groups.

O'Reilly et al. (2015) contend that although peacebuilding requires input from the broader society, "women – who are rarely the belligerents – are unlikely to be considered legitimate participants" in ending violence. Civilian women may be viewed as lacking authority in the security domain especially, which can impair their ability to participate in the implementation of such provisions. Bramble and Paffenholz (2020) argue that, although civil society can contribute meaningfully to security sector reform, female civil society actors' formal participation has been extremely limited due to the belief that they lack the network and technical capacity to contribute meaningfully to important security initiatives. They argue that, in the past, "extremely sensitive processes relating to decommissioning and intelligence reform that affect the safety of armed groups and the security of the state remained off-limits for civil society participation other than the advisory role of academic experts" (Bramble and Paffenholz 2020, 31). When women from civil society are allowed to participate in implementation, they may be limited in the types of tasks they can contribute to. In essential areas like security sector reform, legitimacy is often accorded to actors that have participated in a conflict as militants. While this possibly unfounded set of assumptions may constrain women from civil society, it can allow women from former rebel parties to play a more important role in the implementation process, especially regarding security sector reforms.

Female legislators from rebel parties are less likely to face these same impediments. Given their links to one of the primary warring factions, female legislators who represent rebel parties will have greater dominion over the peace process than female legislators without links to a warring party. Rebel party women legislators can draw on the authority of warring parties to stake a claim to the implementation process. At the same time, we argue that female legislators will be more likely to push for gender provisions than male legislators from the same party. While rebel party men can advance women's interests, we argue that women politicians will be more likely to push gender-inclusive provisions and encourage other parties to do so as well. Though women are not a monolith and, thus, will not always prioritize or favor policies regarding women or gender, there is ample research that makes the connection between women's descriptive representation and their substantive representation (Celis et al. 2008; Foos and Gilardi 2020; Gilardi 2015; Hinojosa 2012; Mansbridge 1999; Paxton and Kunovich 2003; Schwindt-Bayer 2003; Wolbrecht and Campbell 2007). This work demonstrates women's representation within political institutions can alter the focus on policy issues relevant to women and gender (Childs 2004; Dodson 2006; Greene and O'Brien 2016; O'Brien and Piscopo 2019; Piscopo 2011). This may be because women representatives have a genuine interest in issues related to women and gender (Mansbridge 1999), they see themselves as responsible for representing the interests of women (Childs 2004; Franceschet and Piscopo 2008; Schwindt-Bayer 2010), or because they fear backlash for failing to conform to gendered expectations that they represent "feminine" and "communal" issues (Eagly and Karau 2002). Even when they prioritize similar issues, male and female legislators' stances and areas of emphasis diverge (Greene and O'Brien 2016). Moreover, women's integration has been found to encourage parties to take up both a greater range of issues and shift parties' positions on left-leaning issues (Greene and O'Brien 2016). Extrapolating to peace agreement provisions, women legislators may encourage their parties to view a greater range of issues as important and adopt more leftist policy positions, namely those that address women's rights and welfare and the disadvantaged. Thus, women representatives may be more likely to advocate for the implementation of gendered peace provisions when in government, especially when these provisions also align with the interests of the rebel movement and their supporters.

The election of female candidates can indicate a norm shift, which encourages all parties that hope to contend in elections to take women's interests and issues seriously to gain vote share. Catalano-Weeks (2018) argues that even male-dominated parties are incentivized to pursue gender-inclusive legislation, such as quotas, in the face of heightened competition. Thus, we might expect that when female candidates are elected, parties will perceive women's issues as more salient concerns to the public, compelling them to adopt these policy positions as well. If this is the case, rebel parties will not be the only political factions to advocate for gender-inclusive peace terms; the election of women candidates may also affect the priorities of parties that do not share a deep ideological or political commitment to ensuring equality for women. However, given the crucial role of former rebels in implementation, we expect women representatives' statuses in rebel parties to increase their overall influence on the process with downstream consequences for implementation.

Finally, women participants can make these organizations appear more trustworthy, committed to peace, and more appealing to domestic and international parties (Berry 2015, 2018; Brannon 2023). We argue rebel parties' quests for the benefits of women's support can manifest in their post-conflict recruitment and the policies they prioritize after wars. Studies suggest that women – especially in politics – are viewed as more trustworthy than men (Barnes and Beaulieu 2014; Huddy and Terkildsen 1993; Sanbonmatsu 2002), which may influence their ability to shape the implementation of peace. In Rwanda, women were seen as "less corruptible" and more committed to reconciliation and peace, which is part of the reason they were appealing recruits for the RPF (Powley 2003). Similarly, in Liberia, women activists campaigned on behalf of women candidates, arguing that while men were responsible for the conflicts, women would promote peace (Massaquoi 2007). Brannon (2023) shows that rebel parties consistently run and elect more women than other political parties, arguing that these parties use women representatives to frame the party as more trustworthy and committed to peace by exploiting peaceful feminine stereotypes. Assumptions that women representatives within these rebel parties will promote and successfully impact peace may enhance their ability to successfully do so once in office, creating a pathway for women representatives in rebel parties to promote implementation.

Thus, we expect higher levels of women's representation in rebel parties to be associated with a higher likelihood of implementing gendered peace provisions.

3.3 The Representation of Ex-Rebel Women in Rebel Parties

Scholars largely overlook the impact that women within resistance movements have on the implementation of gender-inclusive peace terms. This is surprising, given the increased attention on the ways that women rebels affect conflict processes (Braithwaite and Ruiz 2018; Brannon et al. 2023; Harrell 2023; Loken 2017; Mehrl 2022). Moreover, qualitative and quantitative evidence shows that militant women impact the shape of peace agreements (Krause et al. 2018; Méndez 2005; Thomas 2023) and post-conflict politics (Brannon 2021; Tripp 2015). In many countries, such as Uganda, South Africa, Namibia, and Zimbabwe, women's postwar political participation and empowerment were linked to women's efforts during their armed struggles. Women were influential in Uganda's National Resistance Army/Movement and South Africa's ANC, and this wartime participation has been credited with the establishment of gender quotas after conflict and several other advancements in post-conflict women's political, economic, and social rights.

We argue that female legislators with previous ties to rebellion spur the implementation of gender provisions for three key reasons. First, since rebel parties themselves are primary veto players to the peace process, post-conflict governments are incentivized to accommodate their interests to avoid conflict recurrence. Second, former ex-rebel women's connections to their comrades in arms can offer them influence with which to make demands during the implementation process. Political clout can help them push for policies in line with the former rebel parties' interest and their own. Third, ex-rebel women's own interests in realizing gains for women will increase the chance that gender provisions are realized. Former female rebels may generally act as substantive representatives for women's issues, but they will specifically advocate for gender provisions in peace agreements, as those will benefit their party's bottom line. Pushing for the implementation of peace agreement provisions can help rebel parties maintain their wartime support bases while also helping them differentiate their party from others.

Existing research offers evidence that groups that were gender-inclusive during war are likely to be gender-inclusive after transitioning to rebel successor parties. Brannon (2025), for example, finds that former rebel parties that recruited women during wars continue to recruit women post-conflict as well. As they do during conflict, rebel parties can use women to enhance their images after conflict, as women supporters and recruits help feminize rebels and affect the appearance of stability, transformation, and, most importantly, peacefulness (Brannon 2023). This leads former rebel political parties to run women candidates more frequently than non-rebel parties. Brannon (2025) argues that women can provide these benefits to rebel groups even when they are connected to the perpetrators of violence and even when women are among the perpetrators of a civil war; former rebel parties tend to recruit women who served in their organizations during war for electoral positions.

Not only will gender-diverse rebel groups be more likely to continue recruiting women after they transition into political parties, but we suggest that groups that advocated for gender-diverse policies during civil wars will maintain these policies once conflicts are settled. This is for both sincere and opportunistic reasons. Groups that advocate for gender-inclusive provisions in peace agreements are often those that already had some preexisting commitment to egalitarianism during war (Thomas 2023). Gender-diverse rebel groups are more likely to have ideological beliefs that support gender equality and women's inclusion, sometimes including the dismantling of inequalities as one of their political objectives (Henshaw 2016; Ide 2024; Wood 2019; Wood and Thomas 2017). Groups may then pursue the implementation of gender-diverse policies at the end of wars due to sincere commitments.

Additionally, gender-diverse rebel groups tend to advocate for gender-sensitive policies because women form important parts of the coalitions that enabled their wartime viability (Başer 2022; Thomas 2023). Therefore, implementing gender-inclusive peace agreement terms can help rebels maintain this important source of civilian support during peacetime. Popularly supported rebel groups, especially those that maintain their deep wartime social bases, are also likelier to transition successfully into political parties (Kelmendi 2022; Söderberg Kovacs and Hatz 2016), and rebel successor parties that are successful early on are likely to continue to experience electoral success later (Manning and Smith 2019). Hass and Ottman (2022) argue that rebel parties attempt to generate electoral support by providing pre-electoral benefits to their wartime civilian constituencies and core supporters. The resources to provide these benefits are often allotted to former rebels in peace agreements.

Additionally, extant research suggests women play an important role in legitimizing rebel groups (Başer 2022, 2025; Loken 2021, 2024; Manekin and Wood 2020; Matfess 2024; Shekhawat 2015; Stallman and Hadi 2024; Wood 2019) and former rebel parties (Brannon 2023). Thus, former rebel parties that aim to maintain women's support should advance policies that directly benefit their female supporters. While these policies need not be limited to those spelled out in agreements, peace agreement provisions are likely to be a minimum bar. Indeed, Sindre (2019, 507) argues that peace agreements – and a groups' participation in peacebuilding – become hallmarks of former rebel parties, who use "the language of the peace settlements to further legitimize themselves vis-a-vis other ethnic and regional parties." Relatedly, Acosta (2014) shows that rebel groups transition into political parties to advance the political aims they advocated for during war. Thus, we expect rebel groups that worked to secure gender provisions in peace agreements to maintain an interest in implementing these terms after peace is reached.

Female legislators recruited from former rebel groups will play an important role in advancing women's policy interests, especially when those interests align with the rebel movement's and their supporters' aims. Rebel women may have unique experiences that sensitize them to a different set of policies than other women and even their own male comrades. The process of socialization during war can encourage female rebels to develop a gender consciousness that attunes them to discrimination against those in their close circles, including both marginalized and excluded women and militant women (Thomas 2023). Militant women, therefore, push for gender-inclusive peace terms that attempt to remedy historical political marginalization and provisions that call for rebel women's rehabilitation and reintegration (Thomas 2023). Such terms appear more frequently when gender-diverse rebel groups are among an agreement's signatories (Thomas 2023). When women from within this identity group (i.e., militant women) are integrated into post-conflict politics, they will continue to advocate for these same provisions. However, their need to compete for electoral support among a broader constituency may encourage female candidates from rebel parties to advance a wider set of women's issues as well.

In addition to their distinctive interests, women from rebel parties also have a unique opportunity to advance gender-inclusive peace terms since they are an integral part of the post-conflict power structure. Implementing parties often prioritize the interests of the core belligerents over the interests of outsiders. Therefore, women from former rebel parties may have an advantage over other women representatives, as female rebel party legislators would have dispensation to push for the interests of the former armed groups they represent. A rebel party affiliation can also offer a female legislator the clout to address important conflict-related issues, including those dealing with security guarantees and DDR.

While rebel women are likely to hold a relatively small percentage of rebel party seats (Brannon 2025), we expect that they will be "critical actors" within these parties, meaning that they will act individually or collectively to advance women's interests and can have significant impacts despite potentially modest representation (see Childs and Krook 2009). Critical mass theory – which asserts that women will impact policy outcomes when their representation surpasses a meaningful threshold – gained early attention and support (Dahlerup 1988), but has since been hotly debated and questioned (Beckwith and Cowell-Meyers 2007; Childs and Krook 2006, 2008, 2009), with scholars arguing that numbers alone do not determine success. Women's representation in legislatures may meet a critical mass, but women may struggle to push forward policy due to the political context and backlash (Childs and Krook 2006; Grey 2006). Moreover, scholars have pushed back against the idea of critical mass to demonstrate that even a small number of women in politics can have a profound effect (Bratton 2005; Crowley 2011). Childs and Krook (2009) argue that even in the absence of a critical mass, one or a few "critical actors" can have profound effects. We expect that ex-rebel women representatives can act as critical actors in their parties, even if their numbers remain small.

We argue ex-rebel women can act as critical actors because of their ability to exploit pre-existing connections to their former rebel comrades and other affiliates to get their policy goals met. Participation in an armed rebellion can offer ex-rebel women political insider status that can be used to influence the implementation process. In party politics, connections to powerbrokers often affect both whether an individual is elected and the power they are able to wield once in office. According to Moore (1988, 568), "network centrality is a valuable resource easily converted into influence and advantage." Moreover, scholars argue that in party politics, being viewed as "one of us" can be more important than "policy expertise or formal qualifications" (Norris and Lovendusky 1995, 238). Since success in party politics often requires access to "insular party networks" (Martinez-Canto and Verge 2023), preexisting interpersonal ties can play a large role in determining whether a politician is able to exercise influence over a party's priorities (Martinez-Canto and Verge 2022; Norris and Lovendusky 1995). Connections to the party leadership are particularly important, as these leaders help "determine the policies his or her party aims to implement once in government" (O'Brien 2015, 1023).

Participation in rebellion can offer female ex-rebels access to these important but insular networks that render them political insiders. Since women are often cast as outsiders, they tend to be excluded from informal elite networks (Moore 1988), specifically party networks (O'Brien 2015). On average, women hold less interpersonal capital (i.e., bonding ties), which can make it difficult for them to wield influence over politics even when they are elected (Martinez-Canto and Verge 2022). According to Verge and Claveria (2018, 537), women often lack homosocial capital, which is ostensibly "trust, likeability and familiarity," which can explain why they are relatively disadvantaged in politics. Gender is often used as a heuristic to determine if someone possesses such traits, but interpersonal history and having already permeated a group's inner circle should overtake the need for male leaders to rely on these cues. Thus, the networks built during the rebellion can afford ex-rebel women the influence with which to sway policies once in government, especially those related to the implementation of gender provisions.

Aduda and Liesch (2022, 5) argue that women are most likely to affect a peace process when they have national or international standing. Such prestige enables women to be vocal about the provisions they would like included in an agreement, and makes other actors inclined to heed their calls. Moreover, women's influence will be greatest when women are deemed veto players during negotiations (Aduda and Liesch 2022). We expect a similar dynamic to play out during the implementation process. In particular, women legislators' prior participation in rebellion and sustained connections to their powerful comrades in a rebel successor party can offer ex-rebel women standing with which to affect the implementation of gender provisions. Political insider status can offer ex-rebel women social capital and standing that many other women legislators may lack.

While other women legislators may possess connections to powerful leaders that could offer them influence in the legislature more generally, this clout may not necessarily produce advantages in the post-conflict peace agreement implementation process. As Aduda and Liesch (2022) suggest, veto player status is essential for standing in the peace process, and only actors that can unilaterally resume a conflict are considered veto players. This would offer greater influence to female legislators connected to belligerent parties, at least in this specific domain. At the same time, proximity to rebel leadership will not necessarily help ex-rebel women legislators advance all policy aims; we argue these connections and this experience will be specifically useful during the peace agreement implementation process, as this is often an arena where former belligerents, including rebel group successor parties, exercise control.

Our argument emphasizes connections to the rebel party establishment, but we believe that ties with actors outside of the conflict can help female former rebels push for implementation. We argue that ex-rebel women can act as a bridge between the political establishment and actors deemed political outsiders. Research proffers that rebel women rely on their relationships with other women – including those in civil society and the international community – to set the agenda and strengthen their push for gender inclusion during peace processes. For example, female rebels from the FARC, CPN-M, and the Farabundo Martí National Liberation Front all used their connections to political actors outside of their rebel organizations to ensure women's interests were prioritized in peace agreements. This type of networking would prove useful for implementation, facilitating legislators' ability to foster change. Krause et al. (2018) find that gender-inclusivity in peace agreements is more probable and implementation more likely when there are linkages among groups of women, namely those in civil society, and female signatories at the negotiating table. The relationship between Luz Mendez, a negotiator and signatory for the Guatemalan URNG coalition, and women civil society actors further demonstrates this dynamic (Krause et al. 2018). Mendez suggests that a partnership between the members of the Guatemalan coalition of armed groups and leaders of civil society enabled negotiations to begin in the first place but also allowed for the articulation of a gender approach.[10] Mendez acted as a mouthpiece for women's organizations within the Assembly of Civil Society. The assembly would submit their positions on women's issues as recommendations to the negotiating parties, and Mendez would push for these points during formal negotiations, especially when detractors argued there was no precedent for including such accommodations.[11] According to Mendez, "the Guatemalan Peace Accords were well known because of their bold gender approach. Women's economic, political, and social rights were included in a majority of the accords [as a] result of the direct participation of women, strengthened with gender awareness, at both the Assembly of Civil Society and the peace table even though deeply under-represented in this last space."

We make a similar argument about linkages between women within rebel groups, negotiating parties, and women within the broader society with regard to the implementation process. More concretely, we believe female rebels can leverage their relationships with other powerful actors in rebel parties to push for specific gender-inclusive policies. The crafting of policy, however, can be done in concert with civil society actors, who may be better poised to generate public support for these changes. Together, coalitions of women can exert pressure from above and below, which increases the likelihood that gender terms are prioritized during the implementation process. In the Central African Republic's (CAR) 2019 peace process, for instance, women from rebel groups worked with delegates from the government and observers from civil society to push for the inclusion of gender provisions in the peace agreement. Moreover, women participated in the monitoring mechanism to guarantee the government honored its promises, including a 35% candidate quota for all political parties (UN-DPO 2020).

South Africa's African National Congress provides an apt example of how women from former militant parties might aid in the implementation of gender-inclusive peace. According to Brechenmacher and Hubbard (2020), ANC women were largely responsible for ushering gender-inclusion and equality into the political process in post-apartheid South Africa. Women from within

---

[10] "Guatemala- Interview with Luz Mendez, Guatemala Peace Woman & Peace Negotiator during the Civil War." Women's UN Report Network. January 12, 2015.
[11] Ibid.

the ANC used the cache they built during the war to facilitate policy changes that would benefit South African women. Women's centrality to the armed political struggle helped transform gender roles and offered validity to women's political power and maneuvering. Women leveraged their broad, cross-cutting alliances and mobilization capacity to help the ANC transform into a viable political party (Brechenmacher and Hubbard 2020). After the organization's transition into a party, women from the group articulated clear priorities on gender issues, including a gender quota.

ANC women noted their presence made a tangible difference in the realization of these goals since their male comrades often expressed opposition despite the organization's commitment to gender equality. Some of the ANC men were purportedly averse to the idea of a quota and women's involvement in the constitution drafting process. The ANC Women's Section took on the role of connecting different groups of women to generate consensus on key issues, including gender equality priorities, and to provide oversight of the party formation process and the constitution drafting process (Brechenmacher and Hubbard 2020). They also helped form the Women's National Coalition (WNC), which drew on revolutionary women's vast network ties to women across the disparate political parties and organizations, within civil society and at the grassroots level, to pressure those negotiating the transition to address women's demands. ANC liberation-era leaders Frene Ginwala and Gertrude Shoppe, who were part of the negotiating team during the transition, collaborated with the WNC to ensure that women's demands were taken seriously in the new constitution and in subsequent law (Brechenmacher and Hubbard 2020; Meer 1998). According to Ginwala, those in political power needed to "listen to women everywhere- in rural and urban areas, factory women, women in big mansions, and bring all their demands together" (Meer 1998, 145). The partnership between liberation activists like Ginwala, Shoppe, Winne Madikezila-Mandela and the WNC enabled a broad and inclusive campaign that led to the successful inclusion of women's demands and the implementation of these policies later.

Like in the ANC transition, we expect that former militant women's inclusion in government will facilitate the implementation of gender peace provisions due to these representatives' connections to party leadership, their ability to forge connections with women outside of their party, and their wartime socialization that attunes rebel women to the need for changes in gender policy and practice. At the same time, we recognize that women's wartime participation could also act as an impediment in post-conflict politics. Women's proximity to violence may besmirch ex-rebel women's reputations and pose obstacles for their post-conflict political power. Brannon (2025) shows that, although rebel women's roles in rebellion can heighten their electoral prospects, their connections to organizations that used extreme violence can stymie their electoral chances. Participation in gender incongruent roles may also pose challenges to ex-rebel women at the ballot box. These same challenges may carry forward even if women are elected, lessening their influence in governments. This same challenge is less likely to dog non-ex-rebel legislators in former rebel parties and women from non-rebel parties. It is also plausible that female rebels absorb the consequences of public stigma during electoral contests, impacting their prospects of election. If so, public criticism may be less of an impediment to women's achievements after they have already succeeded in elections, which is where our theory is focused. We treat this as an empirical question to explore in our analysis. If women's participation in rebellion is more often a liability than an advantage, we should observe that the inclusion of ex-rebel women in post-conflict legislatures decreases the probability that gender provisions are implemented.

3.4 Hypotheses

In the foregoing, we argue that women's representation will shape the implementation of gender peace provisions. First, we expect broadly that women's national representation should impact implementation, as previous research has shown that women's inclusion in peace processes is associated with better outcomes for women, such as greater adoption of gender peace provisions in the agreement and the implementation of peace terms writ large (Krause et al. 2018). Moreover, previous research suggests women's presence in the legislature can signal that gender issues have increased in salience, which can encourage all political parties to promote these issues. Thus, we expect the following:

> **Hypothesis 1:** The likelihood that gender peace provisions are implemented increases with women's national political representation.

Additionally, we expect that women legislators' impact will depend on which parties they are included in and which women are included. Women's representation in rebel parties – armed rebel groups that transitioned into political parties – should be positively associated with the implementation of gender-inclusive peace provisions, as female party members will shape the policy priorities of former belligerent groups. Therefore, we set forth the following hypothesis:

> **Hypothesis 2:** The likelihood that gender peace provisions are implemented increases with women's political representation in rebel parties.

Finally, we argue that female ex-rebel legislators, or women who served in rebel groups during war who are then elected to rebel successor parties, will positively impact the implementation of gender peace provisions. Their gender-conscious wartime socialization, wartime networks, including connections to party leadership, and their ability to forge connections with women outside of their parties will have positive downstream effects on the implementation of gender peace provisions. From these arguments, we derive the following hypothesis:

> **Hypothesis 3:** The likelihood that gender peace provisions are implemented increases with ex-rebel women's political representation.

In the next section, we discuss how we test these arguments, including the novel data we collect to better understand the implementation of gendered provisions.

4 Methodology

This Element assesses the relationship between women elected officials and the implementation of gender-inclusive peace agreement provisions. We confine our inquiry to Africa, although our argument can be useful for understanding trends in other world regions. Africa is a crucial region in which to examine this question given the continent's diversity in terms of electoral participation, gender norms and attitudes, post-conflict stability, women's participation in conflict, and post-conflict women's empowerment. Moreover, Africa has been both the focal point of post-Cold War conflicts and among the regions where women have seen the greatest post-conflict societal transformations. Thus, we believe our analysis captures the most salient region for understanding how women impact the uptake of gendered peace agreement terms. Yet, we still caution against making broad generalizations based on our findings without further research in other regions.

4.1 Data Collection

We undertake a novel data collection to assess the implementation status of gender-inclusive peace agreement provisions. To date, our understanding of the implementation process has been stymied by a dearth of data on governments' efforts to comply with the terms of peace agreements. There have been few efforts to code the implementation of peace agreements and even fewer attempts to assess when gender-inclusive peace terms are implemented. One exception is the Peace Accords Matrix (PAM) (Joshi et al. 2015). While groundbreaking, the PAM captures only whether states implemented the terms in the thirty-four comprehensive peace agreements signed between 1989 and 2012. Moreover, these data code only seven cases of treaties with women's rights provisions. IPAD (Prorok and Cil 2022), another implementation dataset, codes actor-level implementation scores for 189 agreements in the UCDP Peace Agreement Dataset (Pettersson and Öberg 2020), but does not include disaggregated data on the implementation of gender-inclusive provisions. Given the small number of observations for women's rights provisions and the relatively narrow conceptualization of gender-inclusive terms (i.e., only provisions for women's rights) in PAM, we were unable to utilize extant implementation datasets to test our hypotheses. We innovate by collecting the first cross-national dataset that catalogs the implementation of gender-inclusive peace agreement provisions.

We use the PA-X database to identify the universe of agreement provisions, as it includes the most comprehensive set of treaties and, therefore, provisions of any existing data collection effort. The Peace Agreements Database (PA-X) (Bell et al. 2024) includes more than 1600 intrastate peace agreements signed between 1990 and 2024, with about one-third of the agreements penned in Africa. In total, more than 400 PA-X agreements include provisions on women, gender, girls, or gender-based violence, including about 150 African agreements. Crucially, the PA-X lacks information on compliance with treaty terms, so we code the degree of implementation of the different gender-inclusive peace agreement provisions in the relevant PA-X agreements.[13] We expound upon our sample and our coding procedures.

4.2 Sampling Procedure

We use version 8 of the PA-X dataset to identify a sample of ninety-eight African intrastate peace agreements signed since 1990 (Bell et al. 2024). The PA-X database includes agreements for a variety of conflict types, so we start by considering agreements signed between nonstate actors and the government during or following an intrastate conflict.[12] We exclude agreements between only *state* actors (as opposed to state and non-state dyads) that attempt to address transnational or internationalized conflicts (i.e., interstate/intrastate), as well as agreements that aim to address localized domestic conflicts rather than a broader macro-conflict (i.e., intrastate/local).[13] Subsequent iterations of

---

[12] The PA-X uses the UCDP Armed Conflict Database's (Gleditsch et al. 2002) inclusion criteria when coding conflicts.

[13] We exclude inter/intrastate conflicts as these primarily involve negotiations between states, even if they address an intrastate conflict. Rebels are unlikely to have a significant stake in the implementation process of such agreements since they were not key actors in the agreement's negotiation or drafting process. We also exclude localized conflicts, which deal with local rather

our dataset will include these conflicts and investigate whether the implementation of internationalized and local agreements follows similar dynamics as purely intrastate conflicts.

Among the intrastate conflicts, we select agreements with substantive terms, as these treaties are most likely to include gender-inclusive terms that could be implemented. Substantive agreements aim to address the primary incompatibilities that undergird conflicts and thus have important implications for women's long-term welfare. This proviso is important, as we argue that female elected representatives will work to implement agreement terms that advance women's broad interests. Our analysis focuses on four different agreement stages as coded by the PA-X, including agreements classified as "pre-negotiation/process," "framework-substantive, partial," "framework-substantive, comprehensive" and "implementation/renegotiation."[14] We do not include "renewal" or "ceasefire" agreements or any that do not fit into one of the aforementioned categories.[15]

After selecting the initial set of substantive peace agreements, we use the PA-X Gender database (Bell et al. 2024) to identify treaties containing gender-inclusive peace agreement provisions. Appendix Table 1 includes all the provision types for which we code implementation. Given the resource-intensive nature of verifying compliance with individual provisions at multiple post-conflict time periods, we emphasized agreements that had at least one gender-inclusive provision of interest. The provisions that we used to identify the sample are listed in Appendix Table 1 under "Phase 1: PA-X Provisions Used to Identify Sample." Any agreement that had at least one of these provisions was included in our sample. Once we identified the sample, we coded the implementation of the subcategories used to identify the sample, as well as all other gender provisions included in the PA-X dataset. The other gender provisions that were coded, in addition to those identified in the previous column, are listed in Appendix Table 1 under "Phase 2: Additional PA-X Provisions Coded." We selected these specific terms to ensure our dataset included agreements with gender-inclusive provisions that could – in theory – appeal to women legislators, including those from former rebel parties. After confirming that at least one provision of interest was present, we coded the implementation of all the disparate types of gender-inclusive

---

than macro conflict issues, as these issues may be less likely to factor into national legislators' priorities. Moreover, many of these localized agreements relate to violence that does not meet the 25-battle death threshold necessary for inclusion in UCDP's ACD, so are not recognized as armed conflicts.

[14] See PA-X Codebook for definitions of these agreement types.

[15] Renewal agreements are those that reaffirm commitment to a previously signed peace agreement. We exclude this type of agreement since they do not introduce new terms. Ceasefire agreements commit both parties to cease fighting and can offer stipulations for monitoring the ceasefire and demobilization processes. We do not include these agreements because they do not address substantive policy issues and often preclude the election of post-war legislatures.

provisions coded in the PA-X Gender database. In total, we coded thirty-nine provision types.

4.3 Coding Implementation

We understand implementation to be government efforts to comply with peace treaty terms in the spirit in which they were intended. In other words, we attempt to gauge the extent to which states put in place good-faith policies and practices to achieve the outcomes envisioned by those who negotiated the agreement. The degree of implementation was determined by examining each type of provision at three discrete time points – one ($t + 1$), five ($t + 5$), and ten ($t + 10$) years after an agreement was signed, respectively.

Implementation progress was generally coded using many distinct sources; for each provision, we attempted – and were generally able – to locate at least three disparate primary (e.g., constitutions) or secondary sources that corroborate the same interpretation. We relied primarily on the assessment of experts, including IGOs (e.g., UN Women, CEDAW, UN OHCHR), NGOs (e.g., Human Rights Watch, Amnesty International, Accord, International Crisis Group), and external states (e.g., US State Department) to determine the degree of effort the government expended toward implementation and the effectiveness of those efforts. We code effort and intent rather than outcomes alone because many government attempts to implement the terms were frustrated by exogenous factors, ranging from public health emergencies (e.g., Ebola) to a lack of will to accept the changes at the local- and household levels (e.g., female genital mutilation).

We code implementation for each type of gender-inclusive provision on an ordinal three-point scale, ranging from 0 to 2. Zero corresponds to no government effort to implement, 1 denotes minimal implementation and 2 captures moderate or full implementation, which we refer to as substantial implementation. We combine two values – moderate and full implementation – into a single category given the difficulty of determining whether a government fully complied with the intent of a provision. Except for clear quotas, most provisions are not easily quantifiable, and thus, determining whether the provision is fully met can be difficult and subjective. We minimize potential measurement error by reducing the number of categories we code. Detail on our coding rules is provided in Table 1 below.

4.4 Coding Challenges

In some cases, it was difficult to discern either the intent of the negotiators or the expected outcomes from provisions. One example of a vague explication comes from Somalia's 2012 "Protocol Establishing the Technical Selection

Table 1 Coding ordinal implementation

Ordinal value	Value label	Detailed explanation
0	No implementation	No implementation assigned when governments made no attempt to address at least part of their obligation. In some cases, this coding denotes government backsliding after committing to improve in a specific area.
1	Minimal implementation	Minimal implementation indicates that the government initiated nominal or symbolic changes, but those efforts did not amount to a fundamental change in the circumstances that led parties to negotiate for a new government policy or practice.
2	At least moderate implementation (substantial)	Moderate implementation denotes a significant attempt to address the underlying issues in contention. These efforts may not always fully achieve the goals set forth in the provisions, but progress is observable. In other cases, full implementation was achieved.
−77	Provision is too vague to assess implementation	Clear expectations for implementation were not elaborated.
−88	Right-censored	No implementation was coded after 2024.
−99	Relevant institution longer exists	Some provisions refer to government obligations with respect to specific ephemeral institutions (e.g., demobilization programs, transitional governments). These institutions may have a clear expiration date or are set to be replaced, and thus, implementation cannot be coded for later periods.

Committee." A gender-inclusive participation provision states the following: "as soon as practicable after being appointed, the members of the Technical Selection Committee ... *may* declare its meetings open for other observers, including the Somali Civil Society and women groups at any time" (emphasis added). We were unable to code compliance with this provision because it enables but does not mandate or even encourage members of this committee to open its meetings to groups of women. In other cases, provisions might decry the treatment of women but lack language that obligates the relevant parties to address these concerns. For example, in Darfur's (2004) "Protocol between the Government of Sudan, SLM/A and the JEM on the Improvement of the Humanitarian Situation in Darfur," the gender-inclusive human rights provision stipulates the following: "Expressing our utmost concern at the current humanitarian crises in Darfur and its consequences for the civilian population, especially *women* and children, resulting in widespread human suffering" (emphasis added). While this provision notes that the crisis affected women, further steps to address this concern are not outlined in this section of the treaty. Thus, we did not code implementation progress for this provision. Only sixteen agreements contained a provision where a missing value was coded. In only three cases was a missing value the only implementation score assigned in an agreement (i.e., Burundi (2003), Chad (2007), Sudan/Darfur (2004)). In every other case, there was another gender-inclusive obligation for which implementation was coded. This often meant that although one specific provision was vague, the state's obligations were more clearly specified in another part of the agreement.

This relates to another coding challenge we encountered. We rely on the PA-X Gender database's coding to determine whether gender-inclusive provisions were present in a treaty document. The PA-X coded categories of provisions rather than a discrete list of provisions; the data record whether types of terms are present in an agreement along with the relevant agreement text used to make the determination. The PA-X's coding often aggregates together what could be interpreted as different provisions into a single category. The inherent challenge here is that while gauging implementation, coders were sometimes evaluating whether the government complied with one single term – and therefore obligation – and in others, they weighed the degree to which a government implemented many different obligations in a single specific area. Our final aggregated implementation score does not distinguish between these hard and easier cases.

4.5 Descriptive Statistics – Implementation

Each gender provision was categorized as either a gender security, political, or economic development/health agreement term. We examine the maximum implementation score reached (i.e., none (0), minimal (1), or substantial (2)) for each of these categories the year after an agreement is signed (t + 1), five years following an agreement's signing (t + 5) and ten years after an agreement was penned (t + 10). Overall, gender political provisions, which constitute the largest category in these data, are slightly more likely to be implemented than the other two categories. For example, at t + 1 the average implementation for gender political provisions is 1.29, whereas it is 1.13 for gender economic development and 1.12 for gendered security provisions. Difference of means tests suggest significant differences between gender political and gender economic development provisions, and gender political and gender security provisions at the 0.05 significance level. There is no significant difference, however, in the average implementation of gender economic development and gender security provisions one year after an agreement is signed.

Finally, ten years later, the average levels of implementation for gender political, economic, and security provisions are 1.34, 1.35, and 1.31, respectively. There are no significant differences between the mean implementation levels across these categories. Overall, these statistics suggest the average gender provision is only minimally implemented even after a decade, and this interpretation holds across the provision categories. These statistics also show slight backsliding in the implementation of gender political provisions, as the mean level of implementation for these provisions is lower at t + 10 than it is at t + 5. The average implementation level does not change for security provisions across the three time points. Finally, only gender economic development provisions see greater implementation with time. This may relate to the fact that economic development is a slow-moving, time and resource-intensive process, whereas other types of provisions could be implemented more quickly and easily if there was the will to do so.

Figures 1–3 display the distribution of the implementation progress data across the aggregate categories defined in Table 1. These figures highlight the maximum level of implementation reached for each category at each time point. Though gender provisions focused on economic development and health have the lowest *average* implementation scores, they also are the types of provisions with the greatest proportion of agreements reaching full implementation within ten years. By contrast, gender-inclusive security provisions are fully implemented by t + 10 in fewer cases.

Across all three time periods, both political gender provisions and economic development/health provisions were more likely to be implemented moderately or completely compared to not being implemented at all or being only minimally implemented. By contrast, gender-inclusive security provisions are not as readily implemented. One year after an agreement is signed, there are an equal

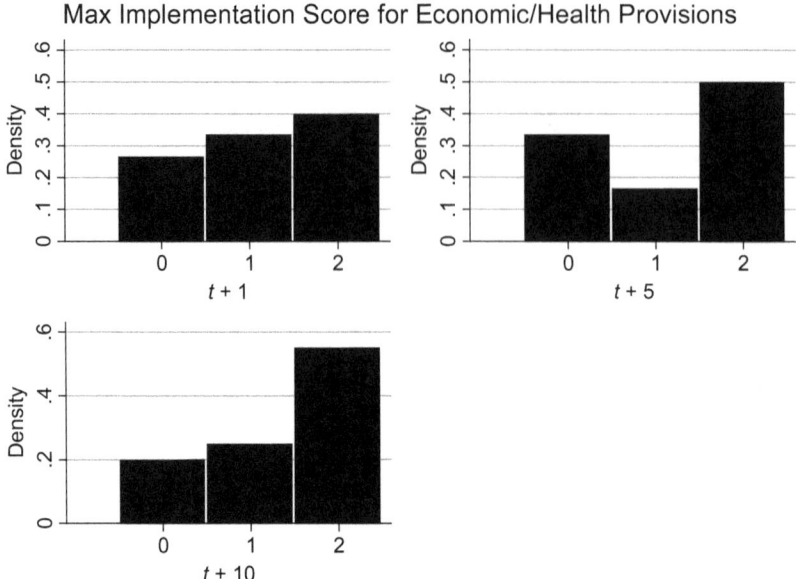

Figure 1 Highest implementation score for gender-inclusive economic development/health provisions at t + 1, t + 5, and t + 10

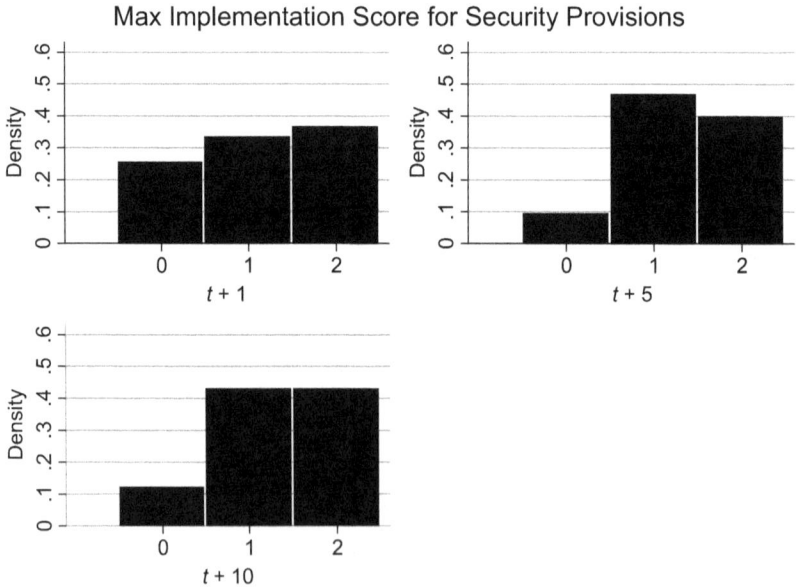

Figure 2 Highest implementation score for gender-inclusive security provisions at t + 1, t + 5, and t + 10

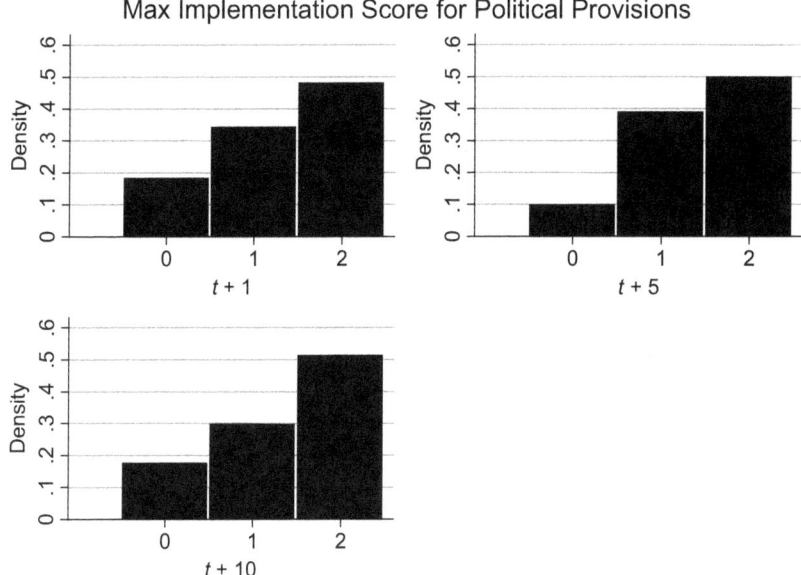

Figure 3 Highest implementation score for gender-inclusive political at t + 1, t + 5, and t + 10

number of cases where there was no implementation progress, minimal progress, or at least moderate progress. There are not more cases where governments made substantial implementation progress than minimal implementation progress, even a decade after an agreement is inked. This is surprising since existing research suggests security provisions are among the first provisions to be implemented in agreements. These data may suggest a notable difference in how states approach implementing security provisions acknowledging women's interests and needs and those that do not.

Finally, the averages that result from aggregating provisions into broad categories mask some interesting variation. For example, ten years after an agreement is concluded, gender-inclusive provisions in the "general development" category have the highest average implementation (1.5), whereas gender-inclusive provisions calling for new political institutions have the worst average implementation score (0.3). Although our research design uses aggregate implementation scores, our data can be useful for scholars seeking to explore differences in implementation across disparate types of gender-inclusive peace agreement provisions further.

Figures 4–6 show how different countries fare with implementation. We generate the maximum (highest) implementation scores by country for each of the provision categories. In some cases, this process aggregates implementation scores across multiple peace processes. Burundi (BDI), for example, is

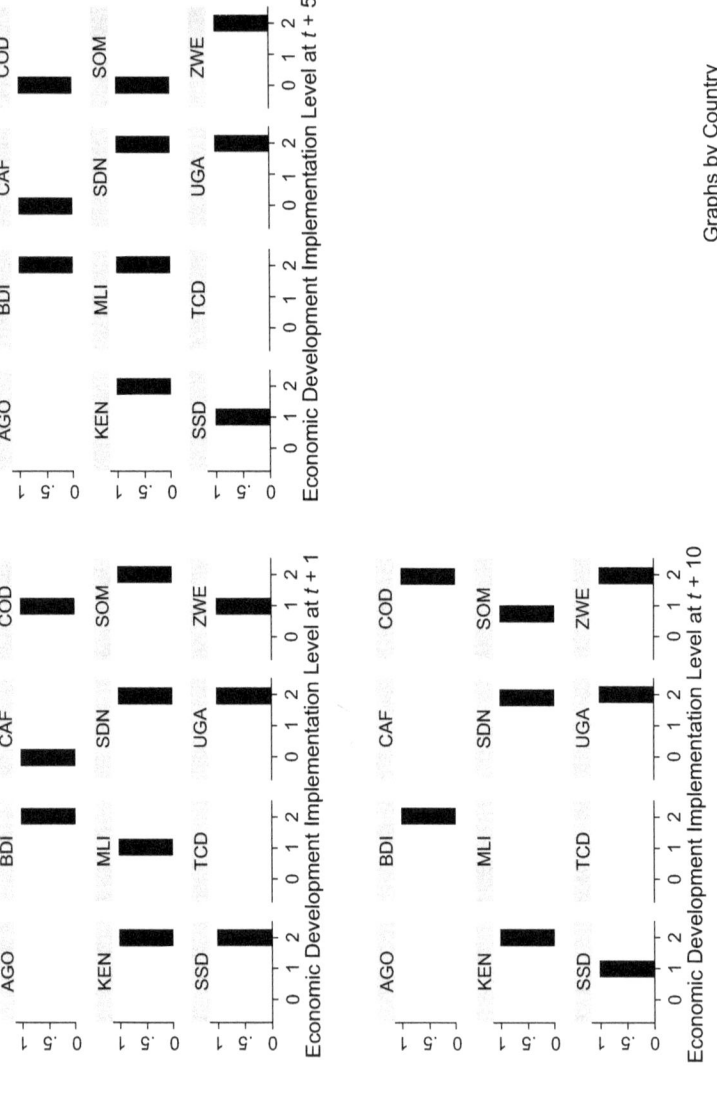

Figure 4 Highest implementation score for gender-inclusive economic development/health provisions by country at t + 1, t + 5, and t + 10

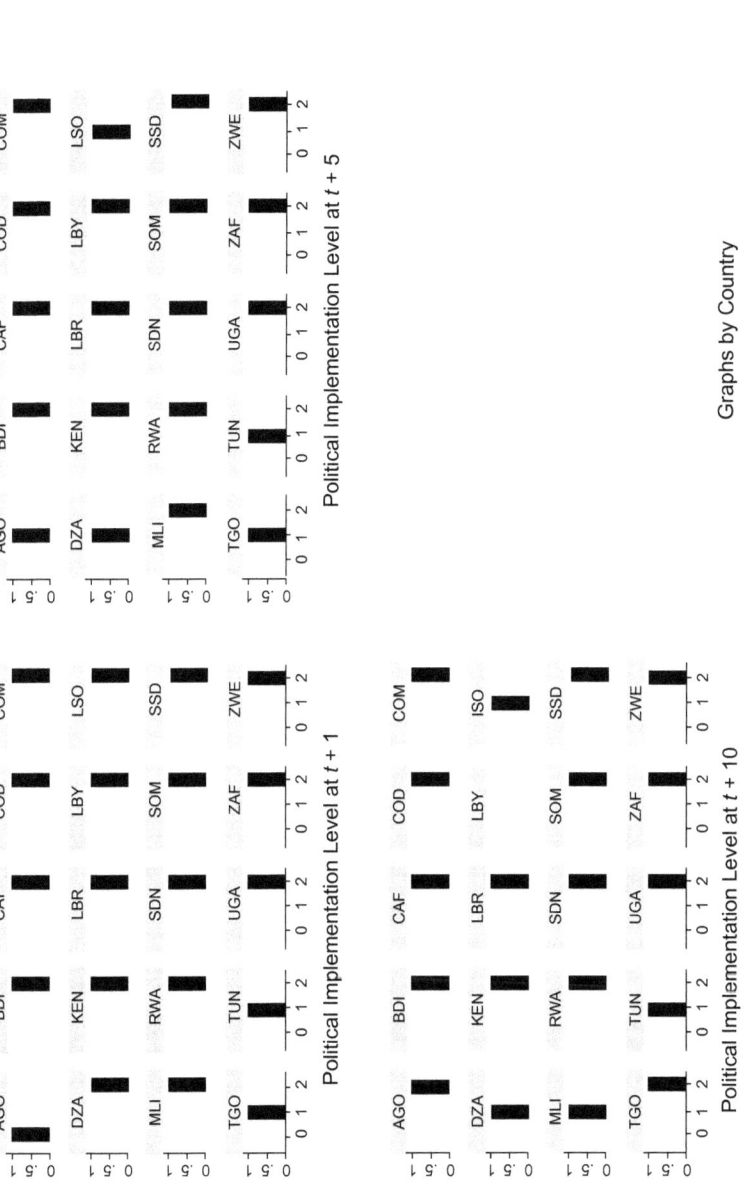

Figure 5 Highest implementation score for gender-inclusive political provisions by country at t + 1, t + 5, and t + 10

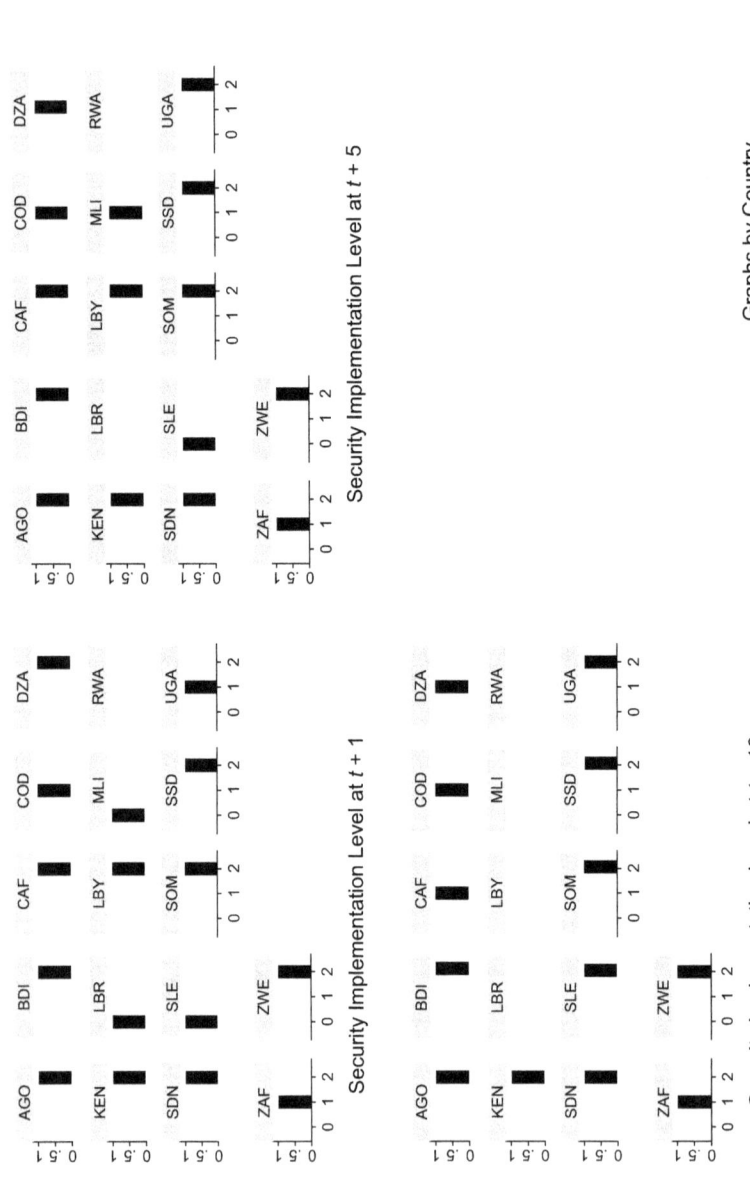

Figure 6 Highest implementation score for gender-inclusive security provisions by country at t + 1, t + 5, and t + 10

party to eight peace agreements in the sample. The Democratic Republic of Congo (COD) has signed nine peace agreements, Somalia (SOM) has inked fourteen, and Sudan (SDN) and South Sudan (SSD) have jointly been party to twenty-five agreements. States such as Chad (TCD), Togo (TGO), Sierra Leone (SLE), Liberia (LBR), and Comoros (COM) are only signatories to one agreement in the dataset.

In Figure 4, we observe that several states made early progress in implementing gender-inclusive agreement provisions in the economic development and health realm. Somalia, Sudan, Burundi, Kenya (KEN), South Sudan, and Uganda (UGA) all made substantial implementation progress on at least one gender-inclusive development/health provision within a year of signing a peace agreement. Conversely, the Central African Republic (CAF) had not even minimally implemented one gender-inclusive peace agreement provision related to economic development or health within the first year of signing. This did not change 5 years after the agreement was signed either.

According to Figure 5, states have the greatest capacity, political will, or interest in implementing gender-inclusive peace agreement provisions with a political bent. Most states that agreed to one such provision made at least minimal implementation progress a year after the provisions were agreed upon. Only Angola had not implemented any political provisions at least minimally by $t + 1$.

Likewise, Figure 6 shows that most countries that integrate a gender-inclusive security provision into a peace agreement will implement at least one such provision fully within ten years of agreeing to those terms. Only the Central African Republic (CAF), Algeria (DZA), and South Africa (ZAF) made no more than minimal implementation progress on their gender-inclusive security provisions even after ten years.

4.6 Research Design

4.6.1 Dependent Variables

We use the data described in the preceding section to code our primary response variable *Average Implementation Progress,* which records aggregate implementation progress across the gender provisions for each agreement. In our robustness check section we discuss the results of models using two alternative indicators: *Substantial Implementation Progress* and *Minimal Implementation Progress.*

Average Implementation Progress captures the mean implementation progress across all gender provisions in each time period. This variable ranges from 0 to 2, with a mean of 1.05 within the sample. Implementation progress for each provision is coded ordinally, ranging from 0, which denotes no progress, to 2, which captures substantial (i.e., moderate or full) progress. Since we code more than three dozen different types of provisions, we collapse all provisions to the agreement-time period (t + 1, t + 5, and t + 10). For example, our dataset contains three observations on the implementation of Algeria's 1999 Civil Harmony Act in 2000, 2004, and 2010. Structuring our data in this way offers us a more parsimonious way to understand a country's compliance with an agreement's gender provisions since implementation can vary substantially across different types of provisions. Such aggregate coding is also similar to that used in existing data collections such as the PAM and IPAD, which deliver aggregate agreement implementation scores. Our data, however, exclusively capture progress on gender-inclusive provisions.

4.6.2 Independent Variables

Our theory posits that women's political representation influences the implementation of gender peace provisions. To test our three hypotheses, we consider three different forms of women's legislative representation: women's political representation writ large, women's representation in former rebel political parties, and the legislative representation of female ex-rebels in rebel parties. We expect that each type of women's representation will positively drive the implementation of gender-inclusive peace provisions, though we theorize that women representing rebel parties, particularly those who served in the rebel group during the conflict, will have a greater impact on implementation due to their positionality, which affords them leverage with which to compel former belligerents to comply with agreement terms.

Our first variable, the *Percentage of Women in the National Legislature,* uses data from the Varieties of Democracy Dataset to measure the percentage of women representatives within the national legislature in a given year (Coppedge 2019). This continuous variable ranges from 1.2% (South Africa in 1992) to 48.75% (Rwanda in 2003), with an average of 20% in our sample. Table 2 presents the breakdown of women's national representation by country.

Proportion of Women in Rebel Parties, our second independent variable, measures the proportion of women elected to *any* rebel party in a year. These data come from Brannon's (2023) dataset on women's electoral representation in rebel parties in Africa from 1970 to 2020. Brannon's (2023) data record the proportion of women elected to each rebel party in an election year, calculated as the number of women MPs in a rebel party divided by the total number of seats for that rebel party. We aggregate Brannon's party-level measure to the country level, given our agreement-year unit of analysis. Our measure then captures the total number of women elected to *any* rebel party divided by the total number of rebel party seats in a year. This is a necessary distinction

Table 2 Female and rebel representation in sample

Country	% Female legislators			% Rebel seats			% Women's seats in rebel party			% Rebel women seats in rebel party		
	Mean	Min	Max	Mean	Min	Max	Mean	Min	Max	Mean	Min	Max
Algeria	7	3	32	81	81	81	0	0	0	0	0	0
Angola	26	15	38	94	93	95	27	16	39	6	4	8
Burundi	28	10	36	66	58	77	24	0	42	1	0	3
Central African Republic	9	9	13	20	6	60	57	57	57	-	-	-
Chad	12	6	15	73	73	73	0	0	0	0	0	0
Comoros	3	3	3	36	36	36	-	-	-	8	8	8
Democratic Republic of Congo	10	8	13	9	4	16	20	11	32	3	0	6
Kenya	17	9	22	-	-	-	-	-	-	-	-	-
Lesotho	24	23	25	-	-	-	-	-	-	-	-	-
Liberia	10	8	13	6	6	6	0	0	0	0	0	0
Libya	16	16	17	19	19	19	48	48	48	0	0	0
Mali/Azawad	12	2	27	-	-	-	-	-	-	-	-	-
Rwanda	23	4	49	62	62	62	39	39	39	3	3	3
Sierra Leone	13.71	13	15	27	2	53	4	0	8	0	0	0
Somalia	18	7	24	-	-	-	-	-	-	-	-	-

Table 2 (cont.)

Country	% Female legislators			% Rebel seats			% Women's seats in rebel party			% Rebel women seats in rebel party		
	Mean	Min	Max	Mean	Min	Max	Mean	Min	Max	Mean	Min	Max
South Africa	21	1	30	65	63	67	36	36	36	3	2	4
South Sudan	24	5	32	22	22	22	26	26	26	0	0	0
Sudan	25	15	31	22	22	22	26	26	26	-	-	-
Togo	13	11	18	-	-	-	-	-	-	-	-	-
Tunisia	28	25	31	-	-	-	-	-	-	-	-	-
Uganda	33	31	35	74	72	75	34	31	37	2	2	2
Zimbabwe	29	15	32	69	65	73	27	18	29	8	4	10

because there are countries within our sample that include more than one rebel party in government, including Angola, Chad, and the Democratic Republic of Congo. Most countries in the sample, however, have one rebel party represented per year.

Table 2 presents descriptive statistics for the level of rebel party representation by country, as well as women's representation in rebel parties and specifically the representation of ex-rebel women in rebel parties. Across our sample, rebel parties hold a high percentage of seats, with an average of 46.5. The highest rebel representation is in Angola at 94%, given that they have multiple rebel parties present. Women's representation in rebel parties ranges from 0 to 57%. On average, women occupy 23% of rebel party seats in our sample, which corresponds to a proportion of 0.23 in these data.

Finally, the *Proportion of Ex-Rebel Women's Representation* measures the proportion of female ex-rebels elected to rebel parties in a year. It is important to note that many of the women elected to rebel parties are not, in fact, former rebels (Brannon 2025). Given the important role that wartime networks and relationships may play in impacting female legislators' ability to influence policy, we assess whether female legislators' participation in rebellion has a unique effect on implementation outcomes. This measure uses Brannon's (2025) data detailing the proportion of female ex-rebels elected to rebel parties globally between 1970 and 2020. Again, we aggregate Brannon's (2025) party-level data to the country-level. The resultant measure specifies the proportion of female ex-rebels elected to any rebel party in a year. Female ex-rebels, on average, are underrepresented in politics, with an average of 2.5% of rebel party seats being held by these women in our sample. The data in our sample ranges from 0% of rebel party seats to 10% of rebel party seats. While this is a low level of representation, case study research suggests that these women can have an outsized impact on politics due to the legitimacy and networks they amassed during wartime (Boyd 1989; Kampwirth 2003; Powley 2003; Waylen 2014).

Importantly, not all countries in our sample have a rebel party that successfully gained seats within our temporal scope. In Kenya, Lesotho, Mali, Somalia, and Togo, no rebel parties gained seats in the legislature, and thus, these countries are not included in analyses with our second and third independent variables. We additionally face constraints of missing data from Brannon's (2025) dataset, which has missing values for Sudan and South Sudan's representation of ex-rebel women. This missingness leads to a relatively small sample size in our statistical models. As a result, we are cautious in drawing inferences only from our quantitative findings and work to triangulate evidence using qualitative evidence. We complement our statistical analyses with three brief shadow cases to further explore the proposed relationships.

4.6.3 Control Variables

Our models control for several potential confounders. We control for the number of gender provisions included in each agreement since progress on individual provisions may be a function of the sheer number of provisions that a country must tackle. We control for GDP per capita (World Bank 2024), as this can impact the level of women's representation and a country's capacity to implement adopted provisions. We also control for UN involvement in the peace process (Thomas 2023), as third-party pressure and influence can both determine how inclusive a post-conflict government is, whether gendered peace agreement provisions are included in an agreement, and whether the state makes progress on implementation. We use data from V-DEM to control for women's civil society participation (Coppedge 2019), as women's movements and organizations are often key drivers of the adoption of gender provisions and implementation progress (Krause et al. 2018). A vibrant civil society may also encourage a greater supply of women in legislative politics. Finally, in models assessing the effect of women's representation in rebel parties, we use data from Brannon (2023) to control for the proportion of seats held by rebel parties within a legislature, as this may impact the ability of women legislators in these parties to influence policy development. In our robustness checks, we control for several other variables that likewise may impact the implementation of gender provisions, including the level of democracy (Coppedge 2019), conflict severity (Davies et al. 2024), and the level of official development assistance (World Bank 2023).

We employ multilevel linear regression models with partial pooled effects at the country level because our analyses include agreements nested within countries.

In the following section, we test our three hypotheses on the relationship between women's legislative presence and the implementation of gender-inclusive peace agreement provisions. We follow this discussion with qualitative evidence that further illustrates our theory.

5 Statistical Results

5.1 The Effect of Women's National Representation on the Implementation of Gender Peace Provisions

Our primary argument suggests women's participation in post-conflict legislatures facilitates the implementation of gender provisions in peace agreements. We focus primarily on women's representation in rebel parties, but we also expect that women's participation in the legislature, writ large, will affect compliance. Due to their typical marginalization within legislative institutions, women legislators are known to collaborate within, across, and even outside of political parties,

Table 3 The effect of women's national representation on the implementation of gender peace provisions

	Multi-level linear models	
	Dependent variables	
	(1)	(2)
	Average implementation score	
Women's national representation	0.01*	0.014**
	(0.005)	(0.006)
# Gender provisions		−0.015*
		(0.008)
GDP per capita		0*
		(0)
UN intervention		0.111
		(0.111)
Women's CSO participation		0.042
		(0.386)
Constant	0.909***	0.947***
	(0.135)	(0.224)
Observations	207	166

Standard errors are in parentheses
*** $p < 0.01$, ** $p < 0.05$, * $p < 0.1$

especially on women's issues, which gives them greater influence over policy-making (Barnes 2016). This propensity to cooperate on issues that affect women suggests that the prospects of implementation for provisions that center women's interests will increase with the number of female legislators, regardless of party affiliation. Moreover, previous research suggests that women legislators can persuade their parties to adopt more left-leaning stances (Greene and O'Brien 2016) and provide strategic incentives for even male-dominated parties to address women's issues and promote women's participation further (Weeks 2018; Weeks et al. 2023). As a result, we expect a positive relationship between the percentage of women in the national legislature and implementation progress on gender-inclusive peace terms (Hypothesis 1). We test this hypothesis in Table 3.

Overall, we find evidence to support the argument that women's national representation increases the likelihood that gender peace provisions are implemented. In both models, the effect of women's national representation is positive, and the effect is statistically significant.

Figures 7 and 8 display the substantive effects of the models in Table 3. Figure 7 depicts the estimated change in average implementation score based on

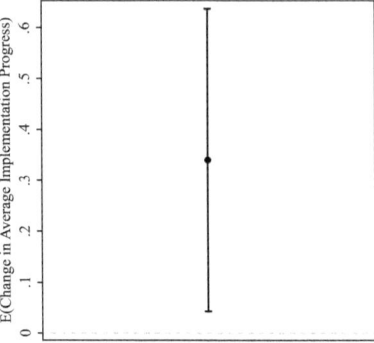

Figure 7 Expected change in average implementation score when women's national representation increases from 10th to 90th percentile, (95% confidence intervals shown)

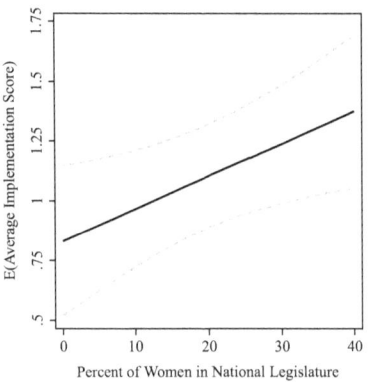

Figure 8 The estimated average implementation score based on the percentage of women in the national legislature, (95% confidence intervals shown)

level of women's national representation. We estimate that when increasing from the 10th percentile of women's national representation (6.68%) to the 90th percentile (31.85%), the average implementation score can be expected to increase by 0.33. Figure 8 shows the expected average implementation score based on the proportion of women's representation in the national legislature. This model shows that the average implementation score is expected to rise steadily as the level of women's national political representation increases. When women's national representation is at 10%, we estimate that the average implementation score will be 0.9. In contrast, at 25%, we estimate it will be 1.15. At very high levels of women's political representation, such as around 40%, we estimate that the average implementation score will be around 1.3. These results generally offer support for our first hypothesis.

5.2 The Effect of Women's Representation in Rebel Parties on the Implementation of Gender Peace Provisions

Our second hypothesis asserts that women in rebel parties will facilitate the enactment of gender-inclusive peace agreement provisions. In short, we argue that since rebel parties are among the actors with the greatest interest in seeing the terms of agreements realized, women from within these parties may work harder to implement the provisions their organizations helped to instigate. Moreover, women elected under the banner of rebel parties will be able to draw from their organizations' legitimacy to demand a role in the implementation process. In addition, we expect women within rebel parties to collaborate with others in the legislature, advocate for a more diverse set of policies, and push their parties to take up women's concerns. As a result, we expect women from within rebel parties to increase the extent to which gender provisions are implemented, as articulated in Hypothesis 2.

Table 4 The effect of women's representation in rebel parties on the implementation of gender peace provisions

	Multi-level linear models		
	Dependent variables		
	(1)	(2)	(3)
	Average implementation score		
Women's representation in rebel parties	0.806	1.023*	0.942
	(0.513)	(0.551)	(0.587)
# Gender provisions		−0.004	−0.003
		(0.011)	(0.013)
GDP per capita		0*	0*
		(0)	(0)
UN intervention		0.004	−0.004
		(0.149)	(0.163)
Women's CSO participation		0.098	−0.085
		(0.583)	(0.812)
Prop. rebel party seats			0.782*
			(0.471)
Constant	0.932***	1.004**	0.802
	(0.187)	(0.416)	(0.598)
/lnsig2 u			
Observations	97	91	73

Standard errors are in parentheses
*** $p < 0.01$, ** $p < 0.05$, * $p < 0.1$

Table 4 tests these arguments by examining the relationship between the proportion of women's representation within rebel parties and our dependent variable: *Average Implementation Score*. Model 1 displays the results of bivariate models, while Models 2 and 3 show results from models with relevant controls.

Interestingly, the results offer only weak support for this hypothesis. Women's representation within rebel parties has a positive effect on implementation in all models but is only significant in one model, Model 2, and only at the 0.10 significance level. We do not find a significant effect in our bivariate model.[16] Additionally, when we control for the overall percentage of seats held by rebel parties, women's representation is no longer significant. The positive, statistically significant effect of the percentage of rebel party seats in Model 2 may suggest that rebel party representation drives the implementation of gender peace agreement provisions, but women within these parties do not have a separate effect from their organizations.

Figures 9 and 10 present the substantive effects of women's representation in rebel parties. Figure 9 shows the estimated change in average implementation progress based on the level of women's national representation. We estimate that when women's national representation increases from the 10th percentile (0%) to the 90th percentile (38.2%), the average implementation score can be expected to increase by 0.39. However, this difference is not statistically significant. Figure 10 presents the estimated average implementation score

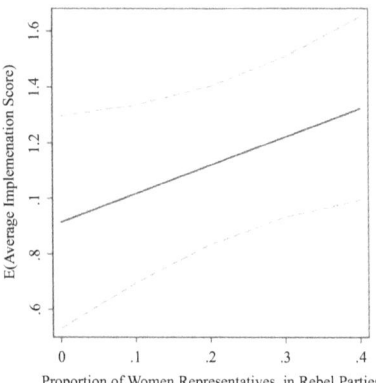

Figure 9 Expected change in average implementation score when women's representation in rebel parties increases from 10th to 90th percentile (95% confidence intervals shown)

---

[16] It is possible that the significance may be impacted by the small sample size. Power analysis indicates that Model 1 has a power of under 0.5, indicating that we are only likely to find significant results approximately 0.46 of the time.

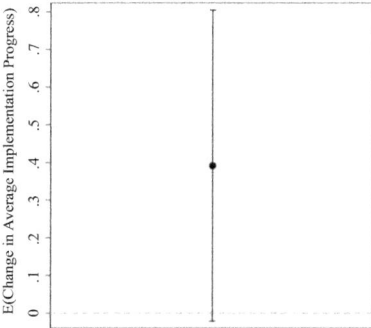

Figure 10 The estimated average implementation score based on the proportion of women in rebel parties (95% confidence intervals shown)

based on the proportion of women's representation in rebel parties, using Model 2 in Table 4. According to Figure 10, as women's representation in rebel parties increases, the average implementation score is also expected to increase. For example, when women hold about 10% of the rebel party seats, the average implementation score is expected to be about 1. When women hold 30% of the seats in rebel parties, we estimate that the average implementation score to increase slightly to around 1.1. Though significant, these are not large substantive effects.

Based on these findings, we hesitate to conclude that Hypothesis 2 is supported. Though we expected any women in rebel parties to exert influence on former belligerents and push for peace, it is possible that the impact on implementation is primarily driven by a subset of these women – ex-rebels – rather than women in the party generally. Previous research has shown that coalitions and collaborations across party lines have been central to women's ability to make progress in peace processes, especially when there is a female ex-rebel present to facilitate gains with rebels (e.g., Krause et al. 2018). Therefore, it may be that female rebels are the necessary link to rebel party leadership, and other female MPs in the party may not have the same influence and networks to push forward policy as those whose bonds were forged during the war. We further explore the role of female ex-rebels in coalitions and parties. Though women legislators' abilities to access and work in coalitions with other women may make a difference, in rebel parties this may hinge on ex-rebel women serving as a key access point. Given a dearth of data on such coalitions, we use qualitative evidence from Angola, Rwanda, and Colombia to explore the ways that female rebel party legislators advocate for the implementation of gender peace terms within coalitions. However, more research should be done in the future to better understand how different women MPs navigate rebel party dynamics.

In the next section, we test whether specific female rebel party legislators are better able to drive implementation. We find, in fact, that women with wartime ties to rebel parties have a clear effect on the implementation of gender provisions, suggesting it is not just the rebel party affiliation but possibly the networks and influence that come from participating in the war that enable rebel party women to impact the implementation process.

5.3 The Effect of Ex-Rebel Women's Representation in Rebel Parties on the Implementation of Gender Peace Provisions

Our final hypothesis suggests that women with ties to the rebel organization before it transitioned to party politics may be better poised to encourage the implementation of gender provisions. Based on this argument, we hypothesize that increases in the proportion of ex-rebel women in rebel parties will be associated with greater levels of gender peace provision implementation. Table 5 presents models testing this third hypothesis using our dependent

Table 5 The effect of ex-rebel women's representation in rebel parties on the implementation of gender peace provisions

	Multi-level linear models		
	Dependent variables		
	(1)	(2)	(3)
	Average implementation score		
Representation of ex-rebel women	5.725*	7.468**	7.384*
	(3.264)	(3.729)	(3.991)
# Gender provisions		−0.009	−0.007
		(0.013)	(0.013)
GDP per capita		0*	0
		(0)	(0)
UN intervention		0.059	0.058
		(0.161)	(0.172)
Women's CSO participation		−0.313	0.134
		(0.731)	(0.963)
Prop. rebel party seats			0.723
			(0.549)
Constant	1.076***	1.453***	0.752
	(0.178)	(0.527)	(0.742)
/lnsig2 u			
Observations	84	78	69

Standard errors are in parentheses
*** $p < 0.01$, ** $p < 0.05$, * $p < 0.1$

variables: *Average Implementation Score*. Again, we test bivariate relationships in Model 1 and include a full set of controls in the remaining models.

Across Models 1–3, the representation of ex-rebel women positively affects implementation progress. The associations are statistically significant, which suggests ex-rebel women's representation is associated with increases in the average implementation score. Importantly, these effects remain even after the inclusion of a variable measuring the overall percentage of rebel party seats in the legislature. We thus conclude that stigma does not appear to constrain ex-rebel women's influence on politics.

Figures 11 and 12 display the substantive effects from Table 5. First, Figure 11 presents the estimated difference in average implementation progress between the 10th to 90th percentile of ex-rebel women's representation. We estimate a 0.48 increase in the average implementation progress when moving from the 10th percentile of ex-rebel women's representation (0%) to the 90th percentile (6.5%). Figure 12 shows the predicted level of implementation across different values of ex-rebel women's representation in rebel parties. As the proportion of former rebel women in rebel parties increases, we estimate that the average implementation score will increase significantly. At the lowest levels of representation – when ex-rebel women hold 0% of a party's seats, the average implementation score is expected to be around 1.05. At a moderate level of representation of ex-rebel women, around 5% of seats, we estimate the average implementation score to be about 1.4. Finally, at a high level of representation, when rebel women hold around 10% of party seats, we estimate that the average implementation score will be around 1.8. Substantively, doubling women's representation in rebel parties from 2.5% to 5% moves the expected implementation status from minimal implementation to about substantial implementation, our highest category.

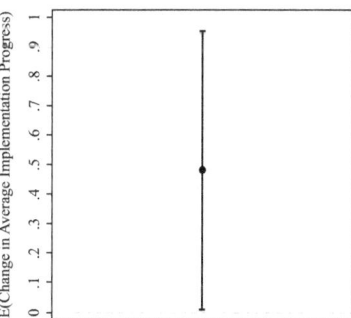

Figure 11 Expected change in average implementation score when ex-rebel women's representation increases from 10th to 90th percentile (95% confidence intervals shown)

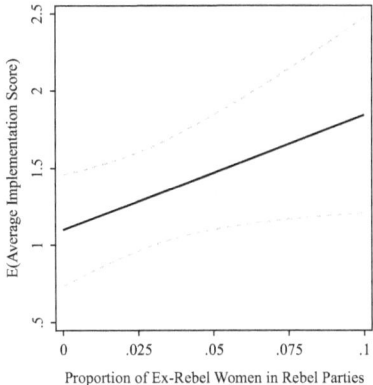

Figure 12 The estimated average implementation score based on the proportion of ex-rebel women in rebel parties (95% confidence intervals shown)

These results offer strong support for Hypothesis 3; as ex-rebel women's representation in rebel parties increases, the likelihood of implementation of gender provisions increases. Moreover, the likelihood of full implementation increases with former female rebels' participation in politics.

5.4 Robustness Checks

We run several robustness checks on our primary models. First, we consider the role of third parties and resources in facilitating implementation. We add controls for the net level of Official Development Assistance (ODA) that is earmarked for gender-related projects. We also control for the presence of a UN Women's office in each country (Thomas 2023). We find that our primary results remain significant. Next, we control for the adoption of gender quotas and the level of gender equality at the signing of the peace agreement. Data on the adoption of gender quotas comes from the QAROT dataset (Hughes et al. 2019). When controlling for gender quotas, we find that the effect of women's national political representation is no longer significant. Our other results are not affected, however. We proxy preexisting gender equality using the fertility rate and the level of female labor force participation in the year a given agreement was signed. We find that our results are consistent after accounting for these factors.

We control for the level of democracy in a country using data from V-Dem (Coppedge 2019). We find that our results remain consistent. We also control for various conflict dynamics, including the number of battle-related deaths produced by the preceding conflict (Pettersson and Öberg 2020) and whether a country experienced a resurgence of conflict during the post-agreement period

(Davies et al. 2024). We find our results are consistent despite these alterations. We consider if the exclusion of cases that did not include rebel parties in the legislature (i.e., Kenya, Lesotho, Mali, Somalia, and Togo) impacted our findings on implementation. We replace these missing values with values of zero for the level of women's representation in rebel parties and the level of representation of female ex-rebels. We find that our results are consistent under these specifications.

We also conduct our analyses with alternative estimators and model specifications. We rerun our models with clustering at the agreement level, rather than the country level, and find that our results remain consistent. We also rerun our models using OLS rather than hierarchical models and include clustered standard errors at the country and agreement level. The effect of ex-rebel female representation on the average level of implementation is no longer significant in these models, though the rest of the results remain consistent. We also rerun all models using alternate operationalizations of our independent variables. Instead of operationalizing our third independent variable as the proportion of ex-rebel women elected to rebel parties, we use the raw count of rebel women elected. We find that the effect on average implementation remains significant and positive.

We also use two alternate operationalizations of our dependent variable. *Substantial Implementation Progress* is a binary variable that captures whether any of the gender provisions were moderately or fully implemented, which corresponds to an implementation score of 2. This variable allows us to understand the conditions under which gender provisions in an agreement reach nearly full implementation. Existing work has shown that gender provisions are less likely to reach such levels (Joshi et al. 2020; Joshi 2025), making the imperative of understanding why and when provisions do reach this degree of implementation even more important. *Minimal Implementation Progress* is a binary variable that captures whether any gender provision in an agreement was at least minimally implemented (i.e., reached an implementation score of 1). This allows us to consider the conditions under which implementation is at least initiated and has shown some progress, and to discern whether patterns of stalled minimal implementation found in other contexts (e.g., Joshi et al. 2020) are generalizable. We find mixed results using these alternative measures. While women's national representation has a significant effect on the minimal implementation score, neither women's representation in rebel parties nor the representation of ex-rebel women has a significant effect on minimal implementation. We find that the representation of ex-rebel women has a significant effect on substantial implementation, but neither women's national representation nor women's representation in rebel parties is significant. While it is possible that different groups of women may be more effective at pushing for specific degrees of implementation, we hesitate to draw conclusions on this particular finding given the rudimentary nature of these binary variables.

5.5 Illustrative Examples

In this section, we include brief illustrations from Angola, Rwanda, and Colombia to demonstrate the ways women MPs from former rebel parties advocate for women's inclusion in political life and advance women's rights. We focus on how women from former rebel parties drove the implementation of gender provisions in the immediate wake of armed conflicts, but also demonstrate that their contributions transcended these specific terms to boost women's empowerment more broadly. We highlight the individual and collective contributions of women parliamentarians from rebel parties and show how crucial policy changes were realized through politicians' collaborations with women from civil society organizations, and in some cases, women from other political parties. Finally, we note the potential limitations of working through political parties, especially when a single party dominates the political system and when rebel parties have little overall influence.

The three cases vary across important conditions in our theory, including the status of the rebel party, support for gender reforms, and coalition building. Angola and Rwanda represent relatively "easy" cases, as the rebel party has a dominant position of power, increasing the influence and access of its women representatives, including ex-rebel women. Additionally, in both cases, there was little pushback against reform in both cases. Though the government appeared apathetic toward gender reforms in Angola, overt opposition was not observed. In Rwanda, there was a strong commitment to gender reforms. Women representatives from rebel parties were able to build strong coalitions that helped facilitate implementation. In Angola, women were able to successfully build on the strong women's associations developed during the war, which served as an important source of coalition building that was influential for implementation later. In Rwanda, while there was no prewar infrastructure, the development of the National Women's Council was an important step in fostering coalition building. In contrast, though Colombia is unique for its extraordinarily high levels of women's wartime inclusion and the high number of gender provisions, it has proved to represent a "hard" case due to the rebel party's lack of political power, government opposition to implementation, and challenges in coalition building between FARC women and other women.

In the cases of Angola and Rwanda, two salient explanations emerge. First, we observe that women connected to both rebels' wartime political establishment and their current leadership acted as initiators of implementation for gender-inclusive provisions. In both cases, women legislators with connections to the dominant rebel party used influence they garnered through their own participation in rebellion to sway policy. Second, we observe that these legislators leveraged their connections to women outside of their parties to help push the implementation of gender provisions further. In both cases, we observed cooperation between ex-rebel women legislators and nonelected women from civil society organizations. In Angola, we also observed cooperation between female former rebel party legislators from two previous warring factions. Although the outcome in Colombia is starkly different both in terms of women's inclusion in the legislature and the degree to which terms are implemented, we see that female rebel party legislators have attempted to foment change through the same channels as in other successful cases. They first attempted to make changes through their legislative participation, and when that did not work, they turned to alliances with women's civil society organizations and women from other parties within the government.

5.5.1 Angola

In Angola, women from two former rebel parties took on the role of advocating for and implementing gender provisions and pushing their organizations to continue following the path to peace. Women legislators' powerful positions and proximity to other powerbrokers through their shared experience of rebellion enabled these pursuits. Additionally, Angolan women legislators cooperated with women from across political parties and relied on partnerships with women in civil society groups to promote women's rights and gender equality.

Angola has adopted multiple peace processes to address decades of on-and-off conflict, including the 1994 Lusaka Protocol, 2002 Luena Memorandum of Understanding (MoU) – an addendum to the Lusaka Protocol, and the 2006 Memorandum of Peace and Understanding in Cabinda Province. While the Lusaka Protocol failed to include any gender provisions or meaningfully address women's concerns for peace, the latter agreements included some gender provisions. The Luena MoU's gender provisions offered a rather vague suggestion that family members could be accommodated in quarterings offered as a part of the DDR program, with an intimation that women would be among those included as relatives. These provisions were eventually implemented (Ducados 2004), despite the fact that rebel women were not well-integrated into the peace process and did not receive their own benefits from the demobilization process. The Cabinda agreement offered a broader call to address women's social standing, mandating the government to "guarantee support to the development of specific functions of families and to promote equal opportunity for women in social and work places."[17] The gender provisions in this agreement were fully implemented within a decade.

Within the first ten years of the 2006 Cabinda agreement, the government made notable efforts to improve women's rights, especially in the areas of gender-based and sexual violence. These efforts included media campaigns focusing on violence against women, increasing women's presence in policing to improve police responses to sexual assault, establishing domestic violence counseling centers, and offering legal aid to survivors of abuse (US State Department 2019). These efforts did not eradicate gender-based discrimination or violence, but Angolan women's status had improved. By 2016 it was recognized that women in Angola generally "enjoy legal protections and occupy cabinet positions and multiple seats in the National Assembly" (Freedom House 2016).

As our theory asserts, Angolan women activists and politicians were instrumental in addressing these issues. The Organization of Angolan Women (OMA), the women's wing of the Popular Movement for the Liberation of Angola (MPLA), was particularly influential. The OMA, created a year into the Angolan war of independence, played a crucial role during the struggle, making up a "substantial number" of the MPLA army (Ducados 2004: 58). OMA's founder served on the MPLA's central committee (Makana 2017), suggesting women had some access to political power and influence in the upper echelons of the MPLA movement. Notably, OMA had a strong track record of providing for women's needs during the war; for example, they made a hostel available to women victims of domestic and wartime violence (Campbell 1998). After the war, the OMA remained a fixture in Angolan politics, impacting the development and adoption of policies relevant to women, including family planning assistance for women and changes to the country's Family Code, which addressed issues as diverse as marriage and the division of household tasks (Ducados 2004).[18]

In the period following the Cabinda agreement, the OMA was steered by female ex-rebels, such as Luzia Inglês Van-Duném and Maria Isabel Malunga Mutunda, two MPLA militants.[19] As MPLA MPs and OMA leaders, they

---

[17] "Memorardum of Peace and Understanding in Cabinda Province." Signed August 1, 2006. https://pax.peaceagreements.org/agreements/wgg/1336/.

[18] In recent years, the OMA has weakened significantly and is often accused of being coopted by the government and having a limited feminist impact (Ducados 2004).

[19] "New OMA Deputy Secretary General Sworn In." *Angola Press Agency.* December 19, 2013. https://advance-lexis-com.proxyiub.uits.iu.edu/api/document?collection=news&id=urn%3acontentItem%3a5B3J-X8S1-DY15-S2V4-00000-00&context=1519360&identityprofileid=KCKCRH51832.

spearheaded initiatives to address women's equal opportunity in Angola. Inglês, for example, has consistently pushed the party to elect more women and successfully proposed the adoption of quotas that require that 30% of party lists be comprised of women candidates.[20]

Other women MPLA-activists-turned-MPs addressed gaps in women's social and economic standing through their roles in government. Maria Filomena Delgado, who served as Minister of Family and Women's Promotion from 2012 to 2017 and the Deputy Minister of the ministry prior to this appointment, led efforts to address the gendered aspects of the peace agreement. Delgado asserts that in 2002, the government had made little progress on these issues as women "had little participation in public life." By the end of her tenure in the ministry, however, she noted substantial gains, including in women's presence in political decision-making bodies at the national, regional, and local levels.[21] The Ministry also made concerted efforts to address women's economic and educational opportunities, including programs to improve women's inclusion in rural entrepreneurship and increase school enrollment.[22] Her ministry led national, provincial, and municipal awareness campaigns, workshops, and trainings on women's rights and domestic abuse.[23] Moreover, Delgado advocated for women's inclusion in social, political, and economic life as a way of peacebuilding, arguing that women's peacebuilding roles were "crucial."[24]

Decades following MPLA's formation as a political party, the number of women in Angola's legislature remained high. After the 2008 elections, for example, 40% of MPLA MPs were women. That same year, which marked six years since the conclusion of the National Union for the Total Independence of Angola's (UNITA) civil war with the Angolan state, a quarter of UNITA's MPs

---

[20] "Women and Gender; A Tradition of Strong Women." *Africa News.* November 18, 2008 Tuesday. https://advance-lexis-com.proxyiub.uits.iu.edu/api/document?collection=news&id=urn%3acontentItem%3a4TYF-K200-TX2J-N0KV-00000-00&context=1519360&identityprofileid=KCKCRH51832.

[21] "Angola; Family Minister Hails Government's Efforts to Empower Women." *Africa News.* April 13, 2015 Monday. https://advance-lexis-com.proxyiub.uits.iu.edu/api/document?collection=news&id=urn%3acontentItem%3a5HXX-VB31-DYR8-345M-00000-00&context=1519360&identityprofileid=KCKCRH51832.

[22] "Angola; Family Minister Unveils Women's Training Centre in Bie." *Africa News.* April 11, 2015 Saturday. https://advance-lexis-com.proxyiub.uits.iu.edu/api/document?collection=news&id=urn%3acontentItem%3a5HXX-VB31-DYR8-321N-00000-00&context=1519360&identityprofileid=KCKCRH51832.

[23] "Human Rights Watch World Report – Angola 2007." Accessed February 12, 2025. www.refworld.org/reference/annualreport/hrw/2007/en/34237.

[24] Dave Bryan. "UN Discusses Role of Women in Conflict Resolution in Africa; UN Discusses Role of Women in Conflict Resolution in Africa." *Canadian Press.* March 28, 2016 Monday. https://advance-lexis-com.proxyiub.uits.iu.edu/api/document?collection=news&id=urn%3acontentItem%3a5JDH-45H1-DY9S-T4B7-00000-00&context=1519360&identityprofileid=KCKCRH51832.

were women.²⁵ Like MPLA women, UNITA women were organized into a women's wing – the League of Angolan Women (LIMA) – during the war. LIMA provided substantial labor for the rebel group, including on the frontline (Makana 2017). Some UNITA rebel women were elected as MPs when the rebel group finally repudiated violence and took up parliamentary seats as an opposition party, though women remained underrepresented in the UNITA party even despite a national quota (Sá and Kilumbo 2024).

Despite their relatively low numbers, UNITA's female MPs have devoted themselves to advancing peace and women's status in politics, like MPLA's female MPs. Helena Bonguela Abel, who joined LIMA at twenty years old and later became a UNITA legislator and LIMA's president, indicated that UNITA women "defend permanent dialogue, the consolidation of peace and the problems that affect citizens that are open to dialogue ... We want more women in decision-making positions as they are the majority group in the country. We call on men to emancipate themselves for gender equality."²⁶ UNITA MP and former rebel, Clarisse Kaputu, similarly linked women's political participation to peace and stability, suggesting women have a unique role in preserving the peace. She proffered that "[during the war] women started to think about things they could do to stop the war and they started to talk about peace ... women are participating more because they know they need to fight for the keeping of peace. Angola has a lot of women living here, more women than men, and women are very much involved in the communication in communities and the point of view held by people ... I think men are ready to start listening to women. I think this country is prepared for the participation of women."²⁷ Finally, MPLA MP and former rebel Luzia Inglês Van-Dúnem asserted that "you need to have women discussing [women's] issues at the National Assembly" to see real change since women have different perspectives and concerns than men.²⁸

There is evidence that Angola's women MPs collaborated with women from outside of the parliamentary body to advance gender policy. According to Mouzinho and Cutaia (2019), Angola's feminist organizers, including Civil Society Organizations (CSOs), needed to form partnerships with the MPLA

---

[25] Louise Redvers. "Politics- Angola: Rise in Women Delegates Promises Change. Inter Press Service, September 30, 2008.

[26] "LIMA Reiterates Continuous Dialogue for Country's Development." Africa Press. June 14, 2024. www.africa-press.net/angola/all-news/lima-reiterates-continuous-dialogue-for-the-countrys-development.

[27] Louise Redvers. "POLITICS-ANGOLA: Ambitious Plans for Women's Participation." InterPress Service. August 2008. www.ipsnews.net/2008/08/politics-angola-ambitious-plans-for-women39s-participation/#google_vignette.

[28] Redvers. "Rise in Women Delegates Promises Change."

government to advance women's rights. Up until the 1990s, this was because Angola was a single-party state with the MPLA at the helm. Even after the expansion of the government and the proliferation of civil society, the MPLA's tight control continued to limit women's activism. Members of the CSO Ondjango Feminista argue that "although women's CSOs play a critical role in exerting pressure on the process of enacting laws and policies, the final outcome in terms of timing and scope is controlled by the MPLA government's political agendas and ideologies" (Mouzinho and Cutaia 2019, 38). This has led women's organizations to develop a cooperative rather than adversarial approach with state actors. Though this arrangement has limited the range of issues feminists are able to address, it has also enabled policy successes on some issues important to women in CSOs and rebel parties. For example, the MPLA government has willingly addressed issues such as domestic violence, even if the party stymies progress on other issues that may contravene its political interests (Mouzinho and Cutaia 2019, 38).

This insight supports several parts of our broad argument. First, it demonstrates that rebel party women advance the gendered interests of the parties they support, though their propensity to toe the party line can restrict the breadth of the women's issues addressed in these efforts. At the same time, it demonstrates that connections and partnerships with those in government can hasten progress on selected issues, supporting the idea that women in rebel parties leverage their connections to powerbrokers in ways that may prove elusive or frustrating to those outside of government.

Finally, there is preliminary evidence that women from the various rebel parties have collaborated with each other to advance peace and women's inclusion. In an NGO-sponsored program established in the wake of the civil war between UNITA and the MPLA government, women from both the aforementioned political parties worked together with other women to identify and solve pertinent community issues and build peace and consensus at the local level. Despite initial skepticism, the ex-combatants emerged as the main mobilizers in this women's group. Grupo EKOLELO, a "mixed" women's association and peacebuilding group, emerged from these initial efforts (Kulp 2009). Grupo EKOLELO women were able to bridge divides first among themselves and then among political parties and community members. They convinced polarized political authorities to initiate joint civic initiatives and oversaw local conflict resolution efforts. According to Kulp (2009, 216), "partly because of their marginalized status, these women were quickly accepted, because the parties in conflict could see them as neutral actors, despite the fact that some of the Grupo EKOLELO members had previously been active in the conflicts." Most germane to our argument, women's participation was central in shifting attitudes about women's roles in society (Kulp 2009).

5.5.2 Rwanda

As in Angola, ex-rebel women in Rwanda aligned with the prevailing rebel party appeared to drive the implementation of gender provisions. They often leveraged the support of women outside of the rebel party, including women in local communities, to realize these policy changes. Their political maneuvering and connections appeared to facilitate the implementation process even though they sometimes withstood resistance from within their own party.

Between 1992 and 1993, the Rwandan government and the Rwandan Patriotic Front (RPF) signed multiple peace agreements, including the Arusha Agreement and related protocols. The agreements were soon made obsolete by the genocide that the Hutu extremist-led government initiated in April 1994. In the aftermath of the conflict, the newly installed RPF government sought to implement some of the protocols with gendered terms that were still relevant to the post-genocide setting. The 1992 Protocol on Power-Sharing within the Framework of a Broad-based Transitional Government, for instance, provided for the establishment of a Ministry of Family Affairs and Promotion of the Status of Women, which was implemented by the RPF's post-genocide government as the Ministry of Women and Family Protection, now the Ministry of Gender and Family Promotion (MIGEPROF). The Protocol on the Repatriation of Rwandese Refugees and the Resettlement of Displaced Persons included provisions to facilitate the repatriation of Rwandan refugees, with a focus on "vulnerable" populations, including women. This also obligated the government to address health inequities by ensuring adequate access to medicine and health clinics. By 2000, the ratio of women dying in childbirth fell by nearly 60%. HIV treatment had become nearly universally accessible, which led to a substantial decline in deaths attributable to AIDs (Drobac and Naughton 2014). These public health achievements largely affected women, as rape was used to weaponize HIV during the genocide. Further, these accomplishments, made within a decade of the genocide, were hailed as a "miracle" produced by the state's "equity agenda" (Drobac and Naughton 2014, 2).

Former rebel women played a key role in the implementation of the gender provisions, as well as the additional efforts the Rwandan government made to address women's political, social, and economic status (Hunt 2017). Notable among them was Aloysia Inyumba, who was appointed the Minister of Family and Women's Promotion when the transitional government was formed in 1994. Inyumba, a Rwandan refugee born and raised in Uganda, joined the RPF rebellion as a college student and eventually became the rebel group's finance commissioner and lead fundraiser. Inyumba's wartime service to the RPF led to her being tapped as a post-conflict political insider. The rebel leader-turned-President Paul Kagame noted that he and Inyumba were acquainted before the rebel group's creation, but her wartime service, including her willingness to go to the frontlines during intense fighting, convinced him of her courage, selflessness, and leadership potential.[29]

In the years immediately following the genocide, Inyumba's ministry focused on rehabilitation and postwar reconstruction.[30] Ministry staff recalled working as "first responders" to the traumatized population – trying to discern the needs of women and families, including women heads-of-household, orphans, widows, and survivors of sexual violence (Hunt 2017, 108). The ministry's early efforts also focused on refugees. Inyumba stated that under her purview, the ministry "followed up women in refugee camps and established a network with the returnee women to bring more refugee women back" (Holmes 2014, 324). For several years after the genocide, efforts to address the health concerns of repatriated refugees were challenging, especially given the lack of aid funneled into the country. However, Inyumba's efforts to improve women's and children's health contributed to the aforementioned public health miracles. One such initiative was Inyumba's 1994 adoption campaign that found homes for children orphaned by the war and genocide.[31]

Inyumba believed that reconstruction progress required women's grassroots mobilization.[32] In 1998, she established the National Women's Council, which created representative positions for women at the cell, sector, district, and provincial levels to participate in local development and governance (Burnet 2008). Though it took some time for the council to gain traction in rural areas, it slowly became a key arm in MIGEPROF's gender empowerment strategy. Women in the council's general assembly organized to address priorities in areas like education, health, and the economy, and offer advocacy and awareness training on new laws and policies benefiting women (Hunt 2017). Looking back on the ministry's achievements, Inyumba reflected that "a number of the initiatives have really become the anchor of who the women are today" (Hunt 2017, 113).

---

[29] Paul Kagame. "Inyumba Was a Very Good Cadre, Unique, Selfless Leader." December 10, 2012. www.paulkagame.rw/inyumba-was-a-very-good-cadre-unique-selfless-leader/.
[30] www.migeprof.gov.rw/about.
[31] "Aloisea Inyumba: A Politician Who Played a Key Role in the Rebuilding of Rwanda." www.the-independent.com/news/obituaries/aloisea-inyumba-politician-who-played-a-key-role-in-the-rebuilding-of-rwanda-8527166.html.
[32] Ibid.

Inuymba was not the only former female RPF fighter to leave her mark on Rwandan politics after the conflict. Ten women were appointed to the country's transitional government in 1994, which constituted 14% of parliamentary seats (Burnet 2019). Rebel women were appointed to other positions of power as well. Rose Kabuye, for example, was an RPF fighter and close wartime colleague of Kagame. She served as an RPF negotiator for the Arusha Accords and was subsequently appointed Mayor of Kigali, where she focused on development and the needs of refugees and widows in the city after the genocide (Burnet 2008). Sisters Rosemary Museminali and Mary Baine, who worked as RPF mobilizers, also adopted prominent postwar positions. Museminali worked with the Ministry of Social Welfare after the genocide, focusing on assisting refugees with particular attention to orphaned children, and later served as ambassador to the United Kingdom and Deputy Foreign Affairs Minister.[33] Baine served as Commissioner General of the Rwandan Revenue Authority until 2011.[34]

Women currently hold more than 60% of Rwanda's parliamentary seats and 55% of the country's ministerial positions. However, since the country remains a one-party-dominant state, most of these seats are affiliated with the RPF or its close coalition partners.[35] While loyalty to the RPF has not prevented female MPs from advancing women's rights, it has limited the policies they are willing to advocate for or throw their support behind publicly (Burnet 2019).

As in Angola, Rwandan women's civil society organizations have helped shape gender policy by working through RPF insiders. The process of changing Rwanda's inheritance laws exemplifies this fruitful relationship. The genocide produced a large number of female- and child-headed households. Rwandan law, however, restricted female property inheritance, leaving female survivors vulnerable. CSOs partnered with the Gender Ministry and Rwanda's Women's Parliamentary Forum to craft the 1999 legislation expanding inheritance to women and girls. This change has been considered among Rwanda's most consequential post-conflict gains for women and girls (Powley 2008). Legislation also made it possible for women to enter contracts, work for pay, own property, and open bank accounts (Burnet 2019). Although the collaboration between CSOs and female politicians was vital for the introduction of

---

[33] "Rosemary Meseminali – Rwanda's Diplomatic Face of Survival and Resilience." The New Times. July 31, 2008. www.newtimes.co.rw/article/10234/rosemary-museminali-a-rwandaas-diplomatic-face-of-survival-and-resilience.

[34] Kabuye, Museminali, and Baine have all fallen out with Kagame in recent years, with Museminali and Baine moving permanently abroad.

[35] "Rwanda Shows That It Takes More than Seats in Parliament to Liberate Women." Open Democracy. March 8, 2023. www.opendemocracy.net/en/5050/rwanda-women-in-parliament-employment-culture-empowerment/.

these policy changes, Rwanda's women MPs ultimately pushed the bill over the finish line by lobbying their male colleagues directly during what former MP Patricie Hajabaka termed a "sensitization campaign" (Powley 2008, 15). Undoubtedly, RPF women MPs' presence and political authority in these deliberations impacted the initiative's success.

5.5.3 Evidence Outside of Africa

We consider the implications of our argument outside of Africa. The implementation of Colombia's 2016 comprehensive agreement provides an interesting analog to the cases we present above, although the observed outcome is demonstrably different. Among many other factors that stymied the implementation of the agreement, the relative lack of influence of FARC women politicians appears to have impaired compliance with gender provisions. Unlike in Angola and Rwanda, Colombia's former rebel party lacks political power and clout within the country's congress, which has limited ex-rebel women's ability to make claims. In addition, women, including those affiliated with the rebellion, continue to be under-represented in government, and there remains "insufficient involvement of women in decision-making processes at all levels" (García 2024, 34). This dearth of political power has inhibited women's ability to be visible change agents, with consequences for the implementation of gender-related peace terms. Consequently, The FARC members that were empowered during the peace process have not experienced the same political dispensation during the implementation process. We argue that this has made it difficult for them to push for the provisions they advocated for during peace negotiations.

Many women shaped the Colombian peace process, including civil society and government women. FARC-EP female combatants, however, were among the women with the greatest influence over the gender approach articulated in the final agreement (Brannon and Best 2022). Farianas served as negotiators, signatories, and members of the innovative "gender subcommittee," which was dedicated to representing women's interests in the agreement. Despite producing one of the most gender-inclusive peace processes worldwide (Bouvier 2016), the implementation of gender provisions has largely stalled in post-conflict Colombia. By December 2022, 7 years after the agreement was signed, only 16 of the comprehensive agreement's 130 gender provisions were implemented fully, while an additional 23 reached an intermediate implementation status (Joshi 2024). Conversely, 70% of the gender provisions had not been addressed or were addressed only minimally. This progress was woefully behind the headway made on the agreement's non-gender provisions. By October 2024, only 17% of the gender provisions were fully implemented, despite Colombia's Leftist president, Gustavo Petro's, attempts to accelerate implementation of the accord.[36] Such stagnation is unfortunate, since Joshi (2024) contends that implementing the gender provisions could increase the treaty's overall success rate.

Ex-combatant women and those from Afro-Colombian and indigenous backgrounds have been particularly affected by the implementation shortfalls, despite the agreement including provisions that addressed the needs of those groups of women (Davis 2021).[37] The reasons for the lack of implementation are complex. Continued violence, right-wing backlash, and lack of government will have all led to stalled implementation of gender provisions. Experts note that continued conflict with the National Liberation Army (ELN) and violence from other dissident groups impairs implementation and ultimately peace (International Crisis Group 2021). Moreover, right-wing backlash to the "untraditional" gender stipulations, exacerbated by Álvaro Uribe's conservative administration, led to early snags in compliance with the peace treaty's gender-inclusive provisions and has contributed to a lack of government will to foster implementation immediately. Our argument suggests an additional possible disruption: limitations on the influence of former rebel party women have also impaired implementation progress.

In 2017, the FARC transitioned into a political party under the Fuerza Alternativa Revolucionaria del Común banner and then rebranded as Comunes in 2021. Like its FARC predecessor, Comunes has attracted women, who are organized into the Comuneras – Mujeres y Diversidades wing. However, as the failure of the national referendum in 2016 suggests, popular sentiment has not favored the FARC's transition into peacetime politics. Hundreds of ex-FARC combatants have been assassinated, with more facing severe threats and challenges to their reintegration, and the rebel political party has gained little traction in electoral contests. To date, the Comunes party has won few seats in either chamber of Colombia's congress. It maintains only five seats in the House and Senate, respectively, as per a stipulation in the 2016 peace treaty. The provision for guaranteed seats expires in 2026. Comunes has not fared much better in local elections, taking just two mayoral positions in the 2018 election (International Crisis Group 2021). Even while Colombia is

---

[36] "As 8-Year Mark of Colombia's Peace Agreement Nears, Speakers in Security Council Highlight Women's Role in Driving Implementation." United Nations Security Council (UNSC). October 15, 2024. https://press.un.org/en/2024/sc15853.doc.htm.

[37] Megan Janetsky. "As Colombia's Peace Crumbles, Female Guerrillas Wonder What's Left for Them." Foreign Policy. November 6, 2021. https://foreignpolicy.com/2021/11/06/colombia-peace-deal-farc-female-women-guerrillas-reintegration/.

witnessing more women elected to political parties than ever before,[38] the relative weakness of the former FARC party has hindered rebel party-aligned women's ability to amass the kind of influence that would enable them to affect the implementation of the gendered aspects of the peace process.

The peace agreement guaranteed the Comunes party seats in the legislature, but did not include stipulations for a gender quota. Thus, ex-FARC women's political participation is not assured. Still, some women who represented the FARC in the peace process have held seats in Colombia's congress since the deal was struck. Sandra Ramírez (Lobo Silva), who participated in the 2012 and 2016 peace processes and was the only woman to sign the 2012 framework agreement, earned one of the FARC's five reserved Senate seats. Victoria Sandino, a former FARC commander and a co-chair of the gender subcommittee during the peace process, occupied a second senate seat (Brannon and Best 2022). Both women served in Colombia's senate from 2018 to 2022. Only Ramírez maintained her seat in the subsequent election.

In 2020, during her first senate term, Ramírez was elected the Colombian Congress's second Vice President and appointed leader of the opposition party coalition. Her campaign focused on implementing the peace agreement. She argued that the implementation process is a "long-term revolutionary project, we have a solid base, we are building unity inside and outside of the party to consolidate a broad coalition so we can be ready for future elections."[39] It remains unclear if she has made headway on this project.

Sandino's experience, on the other hand, suggests ex-FARC women have faced substantial hurdles in their efforts to move the implementation process forward. Even with her political ascension, her ability to effect change has been stymied by the political climate that stigmatizes former female combatants, ultra-right-wing groups, and even her former comrades in the armed struggle (Sandino Simanca Herrera 2024). Crucially, Sandino argues that women's efforts to organize and participate in politics have been hampered by the Comunes party itself. Former rebel party leaders have been unwilling to extend to women political opportunities commensurate with their wartime efforts, political autonomy, or meaningful resources with which to do their work.

Despite these setbacks, Sandino and other women leaders have found creative ways to make gains. These women activists have collaborated with

---

[38] "Recent Elections in Colombia Saw Most Women Voted into Office, Special Representative Tells Security Council, Highlighting Value of Peace." United Nations Media Coverage and Press Releases. April 12, 2022. https://press.un.org/en/2022/sc14859.doc.htm.

[39] "FARC Senator Sandra Ramirez Elected Second Vice-President of Congress." Justice for Colombia. July 22, 2020. https://justiceforcolombia.org/news/farc-senator-sandra-ramirez-elected-second-vice-president-of-congress/

international organizations to establish a national gender training school that instructs women leaders from all over the country in leadership and partnership building (Sandino Simanca Herrera 2024). Together with this emergent generation of women leaders, former women combatants are working to implement the gender components of the agreement, including the reintegration of FARC-EP women. As in the cases of Angola and Rwanda, Colombia's ex-combatant women, including those who had key roles in the peace process, have seen some of the greatest gains by building and sustaining "relationships between women ex-combatants and other women in the communities" (Sandino Simanca Herrera 2024, 13). One such initiative is the National Women's Coordinator platform (CONAMU) led by female combatants from the FARC. CONAMU aims to facilitate the implementation of the peace treaty by establishing a national platform for women's rights and boosting women's political representation at the national, local, and regional levels.[40] This organization leverages relationships between various civil society organizations, IGOs, and government authorities to chart a path forward for implementing the peace agreement.

Colombia's case does not demonstrate that the implementation of the peace agreement was driven by ex-combatant women's outsized political influence. Instead, it hints at the consequences of marginalizing former rebel women from post-conflict peacebuilding efforts and the possibilities for peace if rebel women were able to wield power effectively. It has been less than a decade since the agreement was signed, so its final implementation remains to be seen. Sandino and her colleagues' grassroots efforts appear promising, though, and Ramírez may make progress as second vice-president. With the recruitment of new women leaders – and a space for them in institutional politics – a gendered peace in Colombia might still be realized.

6 Conclusion

Since UNSRC 1325 was passed in 2000, there has been considerable attention on women's roles in peacebuilding, with a particular focus on formal peace processes. This resolution kickstarted the Women, Peace and Security Agenda (WPS), "a policy framework that recognizes that women must be critical actors in all efforts to achieve sustainable international peace and security."[41]

---

[40] "Women's Rights Platform Met in Bogota." UN Verification Mission in Colombia. October 1, 2022. https://colombia.unmissions.org/en/women%E2%80%99s-rights-platform-met-bogot%C3%A1.

[41] Sean Molloy. "Making Connections between Peace Agreements, Parliamentarians and Security Council Agendas." PeaceRep. October 4, 2023. https://peacerep.org/2023/10/04/making-connections-peace-agreements-parliament-security-council-agendas/.

Academic focus has shifted with this policy focus. There is now a considerable body of research demonstrating women's pivotal roles in peace processes, particularly their effects on the gendering of agreements and peace durability. Our Element builds on and extends this research by examining whether women continue to exert a positive impact on peace agreements long after they have been signed.

We argue that women's continued influence, through their representation in postwar legislatures, fosters greater implementation of gender peace provisions. Though we expect women representatives to generally exert a positive effect, we focus primarily on the impact of women in former belligerent parties – those rebel groups that transition into political parties. Given their proximity and connections to a primary conflict belligerent, we assert that women legislators in rebel parties uniquely affect the implementation progress on gender provisions. Further, we propose distinctions between women within rebel parties and contend that women's wartime backgrounds impact their levels of influence over the implementation process. Specifically, we expect ex-rebel women legislators to have an outsized effect on compliance with gender-inclusive provisions due to their gender-conscious wartime socialization, networks – including connections to rebel party leadership – and ability to exploit new and well-established connections with women outside of their parties.

We test our arguments on newly collected data on the implementation of gender peace provisions in agreements signed in Africa since 1990. With these novel data, we find some evidence that women's national representation and women's rebel party representation both positively impact implementation progress. Crucially, we find robust evidence that ex-rebel women's representation in postwar legislatures increases the probability of gender peace provision implementation. We complement our statistical analyses with three illustrative cases of Angola, Rwanda, and Colombia that offer further evidence of women's influence over implementation, particularly when they serve as representatives in former rebel parties and when they wield wartime connections to rebel groups. Throughout these cases, we show women can be a positive force for peace, facilitating implementation and advocating for the adoption of additional policies that benefit women. Each case also highlights the importance of the government in facilitating women's efforts. The lack of government support stymied Colombia's female politicians' progress. Though the Rwandan and Ugandan governments were generally supportive of women's efforts, those regimes also limited the kinds of gendered policies that were pursued and eventually adopted.

Since our quantitative data are limited to Africa, we are careful about extrapolating our findings beyond the region and making sweeping generalizations. Still, we consider how our findings may travel using a case from outside the African region. Our examination of Colombia shows our general argument may have salience beyond the region. Although women in Colombia produced an unprecedented agreement in its focus on gender and women, this advantage has not translated into implementation. Evidence suggests this has resulted, in part, from women's marginalization in post-conflict politics. The Philippines provides another counter-example outside of Africa, where women's participation in the government bolstered both the peace process and post-conflict implementation. The Philippines' Bangsamoro peace process concluded in 2015. The resultant accord aimed to end the long-standing war between the government and the separatist Moro Islamic Liberation Front (MILF). Like Colombia, women played a significant role during the peace process, including Professor Mariam Ferrer, who served as the government's lead negotiator and signatory. Although women participated in the rebel organization, mainly through MILF's supplementary force, the Bangsamoro Islamic Women Auxiliary Brigade (BIWAB), female MILF rebels did not directly participate in negotiations. Instead, MILF tapped Lawyer and human rights activist Raissa Jajurie as a consultant for the MILF peace delegation. According to Jajurie, her presence "signals the openness of the MILF to women's participation in peace-making."[42] MILF was initially resistant to the inclusion of gender terms, but became more receptive after Jajurie rationalized the proposals. Moreover, her previous partnerships with female members of the government delegation on gender issues were instrumental in their ability to get gender terms included in the treaty. The final accord's provisions call for women's meaningful political participation, protection against gender-based violence, and a scheme to finance programs that affect women and other marginalized groups.

Women's participation not only led to an agreement with gender-inclusive provisions, but it appears to have translated into preliminary implementation success as well. According to the International Crisis Group, "women have played an active if not equal role in the political transition as a whole."[43] This high level of women's participation was enabled by a long history of women's political activism in the Philippines, including in the various bouts of peace negotiations. In the lead-up to the peace agreement's signing, women were half of the government members of the peace panel, 100% of the Secretariat, two-thirds of the wealth-sharing technical group, and more than half of the

---

[42] "Philippines: The Women in the GPH-MILF Peace Talks." Peace Women. December 12, 2011. https://peacewomen.org/content/philippines-women-gph-milf-peace-talks.

[43] "The Philippines: Keeping the Bangsamoro Peace Process on Track." International Crisis Group. January 30, 2024. www.crisisgroup.org/asia/south-east-asia/philippines/philippines-keeping-the-bangsamoro-peace-process-on-track.

government's legal team (Duque-Salazar et al. 2022). Though less diverse, MILF's delegation included women who occupied one-third of the wealth-sharing and normalization technical working group seats, respectively. Importantly, peace was on the agenda for many of the country's high-ranking officials, including the country's two female Presidents, cabinet members, supreme court justices, head of the national Unification Commission, and a vibrant civil society (Santiago 2015).

One of the key provisions in the agreement was Bangsamoro autonomy, which was fully implemented when the Bangsamoro Autonomous Region in Muslim Mindanao (BARMM) was established and power was handed over to the Bangsamoro Transition Authority (BTA) in 2019. Twenty percent of those appointed to BTA were women.[44] Before autonomy was granted Jajurie, MILF's female negotiator, was appointed to the Bangsamoro Transition Commission (BTC) in 2013, with responsibilities over wealth-sharing, gender, and development. This commission was also tasked with crafting the laws that would eventually govern Bangsamoro (Santiago 2015). In 2019, Jajurie was appointed a member of the national parliament. Much of her work has been concentrated on building the institutions of the new BARMM government, including the Bangsamoro Women Commission.[45]

The BARMM is expected to hold inaugural elections in 2025. The former rebel MILF recently declared its intention to run in the elections as a political party – The United Bangsamoro Justice Party (UBJP). While the peace has held so far, the future is far from certain. Some important agreement provisions are still not implemented, and violence by former MILF combatants who have not fully demobilized is threatening to destabilize the region. Our argument suggests the upcoming elections provide an opportunity for the former MILF party to encourage implementation and cement peace. Given the Philippines' permissive environment for women's participation and their clear influence on the peace process, women's recruitment to the UBJP is not only possible, but is a logical next step. Further, our work suggests recruiting women to Bangsamoro's parliament, specifically under the banner of the rebel party, will not only increase the chances for compliance with the gender provisions but also reinforce the party's steps toward peace. This conclusion is not only supported by our case studies of Angola and Rwanda, but also by Raissa Jajurie's work in the Philippines parliament.

---

[44] "Southern Philippines: Making Peace Stick in the Bangsamoro." International Crisis Group. May 1, 2023. www.crisisgroup.org/asia/south-east-asia/philippines/331-southern-philippines-making-peace-stick-bangsamoro.

[45] "Member of the Parliament: Raissa H. Jajurie." Bangsamoro Parliament. Accessed February 25, 2025. https://parliament.bangsamoro.gov.ph/member-parliament/atty-jajurie-raissa-h/.

Our focus on women's participation in government, particularly parliament, is consistent with policymakers' recommendations for how states can best ensure progress on the broader Women, Peace and Security agenda. The United Nations, for example, sees the potential for "parliamentarians as gender-sensitive peacebuilders," with MPs playing a unique role in the advancement of the women, peace, and security agenda through their states' adoption and implementation of national action plans and related legislation.[46] Legislators' regular responsibilities include drafting and enacting new legislation, reforming old laws, and overseeing government implementation of new legal statutes, all of which can be purposed for implementing the WPS. Legislators also have the power to allocate resources in state budgets, which can ensure that WPS priorities are funded. Finally, MPs can use their influence to reduce tensions and encourage conflict resolution within their own constituencies. The UN also sees the value of the proliferation of women's legislative caucuses, which promote cross-party collaboration and "focus lawmakers' attention on gender equality and women's rights."[47] Despite this recognized role for women in government, scholars have yet to formally consider the role of women MPs in delivering peace, and both academics and practitioners have overlooked the value of bringing in women MPs from rebel parties specifically. Our work suggests that while women parliamentarians can move the needle on implementing gender provisions, women from rebel parties, and moreover, former female militants from within those parties, could push compliance even further.

Our research has important implications for the broader bodies of work on women's roles in peace processes and rebel party politics. A key contribution of our project is the data collection that enabled us to test our arguments. We believe this data collection will be useful for studies seeking to further understand the determinants of implementation. Though there have been notable efforts to collect data on the implementation of peace processes (e.g., PAM and IPAD), there have been no comprehensive data collection efforts on the implementation of gender peace provisions, despite interest from international governmental organizations like the UN, transnational and domestic women's movements, peacebuilding practitioners, and academics. And, while the PA-X's record of gender peace provisions is impressive, we still lack an understanding of whether the belligerents ultimately comply with such provisions and the circumstances under which such compliance is achieved. Our findings are a first cut at understanding the conditions that foster the implementation of gender

---

[46] "Parliament as Partners Supporting Women Peace and Security Agenda." UNDP November 6, 2019. www.undp.org/publications/parliament-partners-supporting-women-peace-and-security-agenda.
[47] Ibid, 47.

terms. We believe that our research, including our data, will open the door for a future agenda that attempts to further disentangle these relationships.

Through our research, we also push toward a gender-conscious understanding of rebel party dynamics. Much existing research in this area has disregarded gender dynamics and the impact of women's inclusion during and after war, focusing primarily on more direct aspects of conflict settlement and postwar peace. Our findings challenge the idea that gender is not central, however, to these very understandings, and show that women can play a pivotal role in assuring post-conflict stability.

References

Acosta, Benjamin. 2014. From bombs to ballots: When militant organizations transition to political parties. *The Journal of Politics* 76(3), 666–683.

Aduda, Levke, and Johanna Liesch. 2022. "Women at the Table." *Journal of Global Security Studies* 7(1): 1–21.

Aharoni, Sarai. 2011. "Gender and 'Peace Work'." *Politics and Gender* 7(3): 391–416.

Anderlini, Sanam Narghi. 2000. *Women at the Peace Table: Making a Difference*. United Nations Development Fund for Women.

Anderson, Miriam J. 2015. *Windows of Opportunity: How Women Seize Peace Negotiations for Political Change*. University of Oxford Press.

Anderson, Miriam J., and Galia Golan. 2023. "Women and Peace Negotiations." *International Negotiation* 28(2): 157–75.

Bakken, Ingrid Vik, and Halvard Buhaug. 2020. "Civil War and Female Empowerment." *Journal of Conflict Resolution* 65(5): 982–1009.

Barnes, Tiffany D. 2016. *Gendering Legislative Behavior*. Cambridge University Press.

Barnes, Tiffany D., and Emily Beaulieu. 2014. "Gender Stereotypes and Corruption: How Candidates Affect Perceptions of Election Fraud." *Politics and Gender* 10(3): 365–91.

Barsa, Michelle, Olivia Holt-Ivry, Allison Muehlenbeck et al. 2016. "Inclusive Ceasefires: Women, Gender, and a Sustainable End to Violence." Institute for Inclusive Research.

Başer, Çağlayan. 2022. "Women Insurgents, Rebel Organization Structure, and Sustaining the Rebellion." *Security Studies* 31(3): 381–416.

Başer, Çağlayan. 2025. *Public Preferences, Gender, and Foreign Support for Armed Movements*. Cambridge University Press.

Beardsley, Kyle. 2008. "Agreement Without Peace? International Mediation and Time Inconsistency Problems." *American Journal of Political Science* 52(4): 723–40.

Beckwith, Karen, and Kimberly Cowell-Meyers. 2007. "Sheer Numbers." *Perspectives on Politics* 5(3): 553–65.

Bekoe, Dorina A. 2003. "Toward a Theory of Peace Agreement Implementation." *Journal of Asian and African Studies* 38(2–3): 256–94.

Bekoe, Dorina A. 2005. "Mutual Vulnerability and the Implementation of Peace Agreements." *International Journal of Peace Studies* 10(2): 43–68.

Bell, Christine, Sanja Badanjak, Juline Beujouan et al. 2024. "PA-X Codebook: Women, Girls, and Gender (PA-X Gender)." www.peaceagreements.org/wsearch.

Berry, Marie E. 2015. "From Violence to Mobilization." *Mobilization* 20(2): 135–56.

Berry, Marie E. 2018. *War, Women, and Power*. Cambridge University Press.

Bouvier, Virginia. 2016. "Gender and the Role of Women in Colombia's Peace Process." UN Women Background Paper.

Boyd, Rosalind E. 1989. "Empowerment of Women in Uganda." *Review of African Political Economy* 16(45–46): 106–17.

Braithwaite, Alex, and Luna B. Ruiz. 2018. "Female Combatants, Forced Recruitment, and Civil Conflict Outcomes." *Research and Politics* 5(2): 1–7.

Bramble, Alexander, and Thania Paffenholz. 2020. "Implementing Peace Agreements." *Graduate Institute of International Development Studies*. 1–62. UNDP.

Braniff, Máire. 2012. "After Agreement: The Challenges of Implementing Peace." *Shared Space* 14: 15–28.

Brannon, Elizabeth L. 2021. *The Role of Women in Rebel Parties*. Michigan State University.

Brannon, Elizabeth L. 2023. "Women's Political Representation in African Rebel Parties." *Journal of Politics* 85(3): 812–25.

Brannon, Elizabeth L. 2025. "The Election of Former Rebel Women." *Journal of Peace Research* 62(1): 166–81.

Brannon, Elizabeth L. Forthcoming. "Labored Legacies: The Post-Conflict Implications of Women's Wartime Participation." *Journal of Peace Research* 62(6): 1629–45.

Brannon, Elizabeth, and Rebecca Best. 2022. "Here for the Right Reasons." *International Studies Review* 24(1): 1–26.

Brannon, Elizabeth L., Jakana L. Thomas, and Lora L. DiBlasi. 2024. "Fighting for peace? The direct and indirect effects of women's participation in rebel groups on peace negotiations." *The Journal of Politics* 86(2): 507–20.

Bratton, Kathleen A. 2005. "Critical Mass Theory Revisited: The Behavior and Success of Token Women in State Legislatures." *Politics & Gender* 1(1): 97–125.

Brechenmacher, Saskia, and Caroline Hubbard. 2020. "Breaking the Cycle of Gender Exclusion in Political Party Development." *Carnegie Endowment for International Peace*, 1–62.

Breslawski, Jori. 2023. "Can Rebels Bolster Trust in the Government?" *Journal of Conflict Resolution* 67(4): 728–51.

Burnet, Jennie E. 2008. "Gender Balance and the Meanings of Women in Governance in Post-Genocide Rwanda." *African Affairs* 107(428): 361–86.

Burnet, Jennie E. 2019. "Women's Political Representation in Rwanda." Anthropology Faculty Publications. 15.

Campbell, Horace. 1998. "Angolan Women in Search of Peace." *African Journal of Political Science* 3(1): 70–81.

Caprioli, Mary. 2000. "Gendered Conflict." *Journal of Peace Research* 37 (1): 51–68.

Caprioli, Mary. 2005. "Primed for Violence: The Role of Gender Inequality in Predicting Internal Conflict." *International Studies Quarterly* 49(2): 161–78.

Celis, Karen, Sarah Childs, Johanna Kantola, and Mona Lena Krook. 2008. "Rethinking Women's Substantive Representation." *Representation* 44(2): 99–110.

Céspedes-Báez, Lina, and Felipe Jaramillo Ruiz. 2018. "Peace without Women Does Not Go!" *Colombia Internacional* 94: 83–109.

Childs, Sarah. 2004. *New Labour's Women MPs: Women Representing Women*. Routledge.

Childs, Sarah, and Mona Lena Krook. 2006. "Should Feminists Give up on Critical Mass? A Contingent Yes." *Politics & Gender* 2(4): 522–30.

Childs, Sarah, and Mona Lena Krook. 2008. "Critical Mass Theory and Women's Political Representation." *Political studies* 56 (3): 725–36.

Childs, Sarah, and Mona Lena Krook. 2009. "Analysing Women's Substantive Representation: From Critical Mass to Critical Actors." *Government and Opposition* 44(2): 125–45.

Coppedge, Michael. 2019. "V-Dem Codebook V9."

Crowley Karlyn. 2011. *Feminism's New Age*. State University of New York Press.

Cunningham, David E. 2013. "Who Should Be at the Table." *Penn State Journal of Law & International Affairs* 2(1): 38–50.

Dahlerup, Drude. 1988. "From a Small to a Large Minority: Women in Scandinavian Politics." *Scandinavian Political Studies* 11(4): 275–98.

Davies, Shawn, Garoun Engström, Therése Pettersson, and Magnus Öberg. 2024. "Organized Violence 1989–2023, and the Prevalence of Organized Crime Groups." *Journal of Peace Research* 61(4): 673–93.

Davis, Lisa. 2021. "Third Party at the Table: Afro-Colombian Women's Struggle for Peace And Inclusion." *Columbia Human Rights Law Review* 4: 363–83.

Demeritt, Jacqueline H. R., Angela D. Nichols, and Eliza G. Kelly. 2014. "Female Participation and Civil War Relapse." *Civil Wars* 16(3): 346–68.

DeRouen, Karl, Mark J. Ferguson, Samuel Norton et al. 2010. "Civil War Peace Agreement Implementation and State Capacity." *Journal of Peace Research* 47(3): 333–46.

Devlin, Claire, and Robert Elgie. 2008. "The Effect of Increased Women's Representation in Parliament." *Parliamentary Affairs* 61(2): 237–54.

Dodson, Debra L. 2006. *The Impact of Women in Congress*. Oxford University Press.

Downs, George, and Stephen John Stedman. 2002. "Evaluation Issues in Peace Implementation." In *Ending Civil Wars*, Stedman, Stephen John, Donald S. Rothchild, and Elizabeth M. Cousens, Lynne Rienner Publishers (Eds.), 43–69.

Drobac, Peter, and Brienna Naughton. 2014. "Health Equity in Rwanda." *Harvard International Review*, 35(4).

Ducados, Henda. 2004. "Angolan Women in the Aftermath of Conflict." *Accord* 15: 58–61.

Duque-Salazar, Juan Diego, Erika Forsberg, and Louise Olsson. 2022. "Implementing Gender Provisions." *International Negotiation* 28(2): 306–37.

Dyrstad, Karin, Kristin M. Bakke, and Helga M. Binningsbø. 2021. "Perceptions of Peace Agreements and Political Trust in Post-War Guatemala, Nepal, and Northern Ireland." *International Peacekeeping* 28(4): 606–31.

Eagly, Alice H., and Steven J. Karau. 2002. "Role Congruity Theory of Prejudice toward Female Leaders." *Psychological Review* 109(3): 573–98.

Ellerby, Kara. 2013. "(En)Gendered Security?" *International Interactions* 39(4): 435–60.

Ellerby, Kara. 2016. "A Seat at the Table Is Not Enough." *Peacebuilding* 4(2): 136–50.

Foos, Florian, and Fabrizio Gilardi. 2020. "Does Exposure to Gender Role Models Increase Women's Political Ambition?" *Journal of Experimental Political Science* 7(3): 157–66.

Fortna, Virginia Page. 2003. "Scraps of Paper?" *International Organization* 57(2): 337–72.

Franceschet, Susan, and Jennifer M. Piscopo. 2008. "Gender Quotas and Women's Substantive Representation." *Politics and Gender* 4(3): 393–425.

Freedom House. 2016. *Freedom in the World 2016 – Angola*.

García, Camila. 2024. "Gender Perspective in the Making." *Global Policy* 15: 26–38.

Geisler, Gisela. 2000. "Parliament Is Another Terrain of Struggle." *The Journal of Modern African Studies* 38(4): 605–30.

Gilardi, Fabrizio. 2015. "The Temporary Importance of Role Models for Women's Political Representation." *American Journal of Political Science* 59(4): 957–70.

Gleditsch, Peter Nils, Mikael Eriksson, Håvard Strand, Meredith Reed Sarkees, and Dan Smith. 2002. "Armed Conflict 1946 –." *Journal of Peace Research* 39(5): 615–37.

Good, Elizabeth. 2025. "Power Over presence: Women's representation in comprehensive peace negotiations and gender provision outcomes." *American Political Science Review* 119(3): 1099–1114.

Government of Sudan, Sudan Liberation Movement/Army, and Justice and Equality Movement. 2004. "Protocol between the Government of Sudan, SLM/A and the JEM on the Improvement of the Humanitarian Situation in Darfur."

Greene, Zachary, and Diana Z. O'Brien. 2016. "Diverse Parties, Diverse Agendas?" *European Journal of Political Research* 55(3): 435–53.

Grey, Sandra. 2006. "Numbers and beyond: The Relevance of Critical Mass in Gender Research." *Politics & Gender* 2(4): 492–502.

Harrell, Baylee. 2023. "Can't Live with Them or Can't Live without Them?" *International Interactions* 49(6): 1–29.

Hartzell, Caroline, and Matthew Hoddie. 2003. "Institutionalizing Peace: Power Sharing and Post-Civil War Conflict Management." *American Journal of Political Science* 47(2): 318–32.

Hass, Felix, and Martin Ottmann. 2022. "The Effect of Wartime Legacies on Electoral Mobilization after Civil War." *Journal of Politics* 84(3): 1322–36.

Hassim, Shireen. 2002. "A Conspiracy of Women." *Social Research: An International Quarterly* 69(3): 693–732.

Henshaw, Alexis Leanna. 2016. "Where Women Rebel." *International Feminist Journal of Politics* 18(1): 39–60.

Hinojosa, Magda. 2012. *Selecting Women, Electing Women*. Temple University Press.

Hirblinger, Andreas, Suzanne Van Hooff, Molly Kellogg, and Thania Paffenholz. 2019. "Supporting or Resisting Change: Elite Strategies in War to Peace and Political Transitions." Inclusive Peace and Transition Initiative.

Hoddie, Matthew, and Caroline Hartzell. 2005. "Signals of Reconciliation: Institution-Building and the Resolution of Civil Wars." *International Studies Review* 7(1): 21–40.

Hogg, Carey Leigh. 2009. "Women's Political Representation in Post-Conflict Rwanda." *Journal of International Women's Studies* 11(3): 34–55.

Holmes, Georgina. 2014. "Gendering the Rwanda Defence Force." *Journal of Intervention and Statebuilding* 8(4): 321–33.

Huddy, Leonie, and Nayda Terkildsen. 1993. "Gender Stereotypes and the Perception of Male and Female Candidates." *American Journal of Political Science* 37(1): 119–47.

Hughes, M. M., Paxton, P., Clayton, A. B., & Zetterberg, P. 2019. Global gender quota adoption, implementation, and reform. Comparative Politics, 51(2), 219–38.

Hunt, Swanee. 2017. *Rwandan Women Rising*. Duke University Press.

Ide, Tobias. 2024. "Supply and Demand: Drivers of Women Non-Combat Participation in Rebel Groups." *Studies in Conflict & Terrorism*: 1–19.

International Crisis Group. 2021. "A Fight by Other Means." November 30.

Ishiyama, John, and Anna Batta. 2011. "Swords into Plowshares." *Communist and Post-Communist Studies* 44(4): 369–79.

Ishiyama, John, and Michael Widmeier. 2020. "From 'Bush Bureaucracies' to Electoral Competition." *Journal of Elections, Public Opinion and Parties* 30(1): 42–63.

Itto, Anne. 2006. "Guests at the Table? The Role of Women in Peace Processes." *Peace by Piece* 18: 56–59.

Jarstad, Anna K., and Desiree Nilsson. 2008. "From Words to Deeds." *Conflict Management and Peace Science* 25(3): 206–23.

Johnson, Chelsea. 2021. "Power-Sharing, Conflict Resolution, and the Logic of Pre-Emptive Defection." *Journal of Peace Research* 58(4): 734–48.

Johnson, Chelsea. 2023. "Political Power Sharing in Post-Conflict Democracies." *Democratization* 30(6): 1135–59.

Joo, Minnie M. 2025. "Resolving Bargaining Problems in Civil Conflicts." *Journal of Peace Research* 62(3): 722–37.

Joshi, Madhav. 2024. "Does the Implementation Status of Gender Provisions Affect the Implementation of a Peace Agreement?" *Policy Studies Journal* 53: 1152–63.

Joshi, Madhav. 2025. "Civil war induced social rupture and transformative changes: Women's political participation and land ownership in post-war Nepal." International Journal of Politics, Culture, and Society: 1–35.

Joshi, Madhav, Sung Yong Lee, and Roger Mac Ginty. 2017. "Built-in Safeguards and the Implementation of Civil War Peace Accords." *International Interactions* 43(6): 994–1018.

Joshi, Madhav, and T. David Mason. 2011. "Civil War Settlements, Size of Governing Coalition, and Durability of Peace in Post–Civil War States." *International Interactions* 37(4): 388–413.

Joshi, Madhav, Erik Melander, and Jason Michael Quinn. 2017. "Sequencing the Peace." *Journal of Conflict Resolution* 61(1): 4–28.

Joshi, Madhav, Louise Olsson, Rebecca Gindele, Josefina Echavarria Alvarez, and Patrick McQuestion. 2020. Women, Peace and Security: Understanding the Implementation of Gender Stipulations in Peace Agreements, Joint Brief Series: New Insights on Women, Peace and Security (WPS) for the Next Decade, Stockholm: Folke Bernadotte Academy, PRIO and UN Women.

Joshi, Madhav, and J. Michael Quinn. 2015. "Is the Sum Greater than the Parts?" *Negotiation Journal* 31(1): 7–30.

Joshi, Madhav, and Jason Michael Quinn. 2016. "Watch and Learn: Spillover Effects of Peace Accord Implementation on Non-Signatory Armed Groups." *Research and Politics* 3(1): 1–7.

Joshi, Madhav, and Jason Michael Quinn. 2017. "Implementing the Peace." *British Journal of Political Science* 47(4): 869–92.

Joshi, Madhav, Jason Michael Quinn, and Patrick M. Regan. 2015. "Annualized Implementation Data on Comprehensive Intrastate Peace Accords, 1989–2012." *Journal of Peace Research* 52(4): 551–62.

Joshi, Madhav, and Peter Wallensteen. 2018. *Understanding Quality Peace*. Routledge.

Kampwirth, Karen. 2003. *Feminism and the Legacy of Revolution*. Ohio University Press.

Karreth, Johannes, Jason Quinn, Madhav Joshi, and Jaroslav Tir. 2019. "IGOs and the Implementation of Comprehensive Peace Agreements."

Katto, Jonna. 2014. "Landscapes of Belonging." *Journal of Southern African Studies* 40(3): 539–57.

Kelmendi, Pëllumb. 2022. "Rebel Successor Parties and Their Electoral Performance in the Balkans." *Security Studies* 31(3): 446–82.

Kew, Darren, and Anthony Wanis-St John. 2008. "Civil society and peace negotiations: Confronting exclusion." International Negotiation 13(1): 11–36.

Krause, Jana, Werner Krause, and Piia Bränfors. 2018. "Women's Participation in Peace Negotiations and the Durability of Peace." *International Interactions* 44(6): 985–1016.

Kulp, Heather. 2009. "Gender Mainstreaming in Peacebuilding." In Zelizer, Craig, and Robert A. Rubinstein (Eds.), *Building Peace*. Kumarian Press. 203–223.

Loken, Meredith. 2017. "Rethinking Rape." *Security Studies* 26(1): 60–92.

Loken, Meredith. 2021. "Both Needed and Threatened." *Security Dialogue* 52(1): 21–44.

Loken, Meredith. 2024. *Women, Gender, and Rebel Governance during Civil Wars*. Cambridge University Press.

Lyons, Terrence. 2015. "Successful Peace Implementation: Plans and Processes." *Peacebuilding* 4(1): 71–82.

Lyons, Terrence. 2016a. "Successful Peace Implementation." *Peacebuilding* 4(1): 71–82.

Lyons, Terrence. 2016b. "Victorious Rebels and Postwar Politics." *Civil Wars* 18(2): 160–74.

Mageza-Barthel, Rirhandu. 2016. *Mobilizing Transnational Gender Politics in Post-Genocide Rwanda*. Routledge.

Makana, Selina. 2017. "Motherhood as Activism in the Angolan People's War, 1961–1975." *Meridians* 15(2): 353–81.

Manekin, Devorah, and Reed M. Wood. 2020. "Framing the Narrative." *Journal of Conflict Resolution* 64(9): 1–28.

Manning, Carrie. 2004. "Armed Opposition Groups into Political Parties: Comparing Bosnia, Kosovo, and Mozambique." *Studies in Comparative International Development* 39(1): 54–76.

Manning, Carrie. 2007. "Party-Building on the Heels of War." *Democratization* 14(2): 253–72.

Manning, Carrie, and Ian Smith. 2019. "Electoral Performance by Post-Rebel Parties." *Government and Opposition* 54(3): 415–53.

Manning, Carrie, Ian O. Smith, and Ozlem Tuncel. 2024. "Rebels with a Cause: Introducing the Post-rebel Electoral Parties Dataset." *Journal of Peace Research* 61(2): 294–303.

Mansbridge, Jane. 1999. "Should Blacks Represent Blacks and Women Represent Women? A Contingent 'Yes'." *The Journal of Politics* 61(3): 628–57.

Marshall, Michael Christopher, and John Ishiyama. 2018. "Does Political Inclusion of Rebel Parties Promote Peace after Civil Conflict?" In *From Bullets to Ballots*, John Ishiyama (Ed.). Routledge, 41–57.

Martínez-Cantó, Javier, and Tania Verge. 2023. "Interpersonal Resources and Insider/Outsider Dynamics in Party Office." *Comparative Political Studies* 56(1): 131–57.

Massaquoi, William N. 2007. "Women and Post-Conflict Development." *Thesis*. Massachusetts Institute of Technology.

Matanock, Aila M. 2017. "Bullets for Ballots: Electoral Participation Provisions and Enduring Peace After Civil Conflict." *International Security* 41(4), 93–132.

Matanock, Aila M. 2018. "External Engagement." *International Studies Quarterly* 62(3): 656–70.

Matfess, Hilary. 2024. *In Love and at War*. Cambridge University Press.

Mattes, Michaela, and Burcu Savun. 2009. "Fostering Peace after Civil War." *International Studies Quarterly* 53(3): 737–59.

McManus, Jean. (2022). Executive Summary, Five Years After the Signing of the Colombian Final Agreement: Reflections from Implementation Monitoring (Version 1). University of Notre Dame.

Meer, Shamim. 1998. *Women Speak: Reflections on Our Struggles, 1982–1997*. Kwela Books.

Mehrl, Marius. 2022. "Female Combatants and Rebel Group Behaviour: Evidence from Nepal." *Conflict Management and Peace Science* 40(3), 260–80.

Melander, Erik. 2005a. "Gender Equality and Intrastate Armed Conflict." *International Studies Quarterly* 49(4): 695–714.

Melander, Erik. 2005b. "Political Gender Equality and State Human Rights Abuse." *Journal of Peace Research* 42(2): 149–66.

Méndez, Luz. 2005. "Women's Role in Peacemaking: Personal Experiences." In Durham, Helen, and Tracey Gurd (Eds.), *Listening to the Silences: Women and War*, Brill, 43–49.

Mockinlay, John, John Darby, and Roger MacGinty. 2005. "Contemporary Peacemaking: Conflict, Violence and Peace Processes." *International Journal* 60: 884–886.

Molloy, Sean, and Christine Bell. 2019. "How Peace Agreements Provide for Implementation." *Political Settlements Research Programme*:1–47.

Moore, Gwen. 1988. "Women in Elite Positions: Insiders or Outsiders?" *Sociological Forum* 3(4): 566–85. Dordrecht: Kluwer Academic.

Mouzinho, Âurea, and Sizaltina Cutaia. 2019. "Reflections on Feminist Organising in Angola." *Feminist Africa* 33: 33–51.

Mukherjee, Bumba. 2006. "Why Political Power-Sharing Agreements Lead to Enduring Peaceful Resolution of Some Civil Wars, but Not Others?" *International Studies Quarterly* 50(2): 479–504.

Norris, Pippa, and Joni Lovenduski. 1995. *Political Recruitment*. Cambridge University Press.

O'Brien, Diana Z. 2015. "Rising to the Top." *American Journal of Political Science* 59(4): 1022–1039.

O'Brien, Diana, and Jennifer Piscopo. 2019. "The Impact of Women in Parliament." *The Palgrave Handbook of Women's Political Rights*: 53–72.

Olson Lounsbery, Marie, Nicole Gerring, and Kaitlyn Rose. 2024. "Civil War Peace Agreements and Gender Inclusion." *Defence And Peace Economics* 35(1): 86–108.

O'Reilly, Marie, Andrea Ó Súilleabháin, and Thania Paffenholz. 2015. "Reimagining Peacemaking." (June).

Ozcelik, Asli. 2020. "Entrenching Peace in Law." *Melbourne Journal of International Law* 21(1): 190–229.

Paffenholz, Thania, Nick Ross, Steven Dixon, Anna-Lena Schluchter, and Jacqui True. 2016. "Making Women Count, Not Just Counting Women." Geneva: Inclusive Peace and Transition Initiative (The Graduate Institute of International and Development Studies). UN Women.

Pavarti. 2005. "Women in the People's War in Nepal." *Economic and Political Weekly* 40(50): 5234–36.

Paxton, Pamela, and Sheri Kunovich. 2003. "Women's Political Representation." *Social Forces* 82(1): 87–114.

Pechenkina, Anna O., and Jakana L. Thomas. 2020. "Battle Stalemates and Rebel Negotiation Attempts in Civil Wars." *Security Studies* 29(1): 64–91.

Pettersson, Thérése, and Magnus Öberg. 2020. "Organized Violence, 1989–2019." *Journal of Peace Research* 57(4): 597–613.

Piscopo, Jennifer M. 2011. "Rethinking Descriptive Representation." *Parliamentary Affairs* 64(3): 448–72.

Powley, Elizabeth. 2003. *Strengthening Governance: The Role of Women in Rwanda's Transition*. Women Waging Peace.

Powley, Elizabeth. 2008. *Defending Children's Rights*: Defending children's rights: The legislative priorities of Rwandan women parliamentarians. Initiative for Inclusive Security.

Prorok, Alyssa K., and Deniz Cil. 2022. "Cheap Talk or Costly Commitment? Leader Statements and the Implementation of Civil War Peace Agreements." *Journal of Peace Research* 59(3): 409–24.

Reid, Lindsay. 2021. "Peace Agreements and Women's Political Rights Following Civil War." *Journal of Peace Research* 58(6), 1224–38.

Roeder, Phillip, and Donald Rothchild. 2005. *Sustainable Peace*. Cornell University Press.

Ross, Nick. 2017. "Civil Society's Role in Monitoring and Verifying Peace Agreements: Seven Lessons from International Experiences" Geneva: Inclusive Peace & Transition Initiative (The Graduate Institute of International and Development Studies).

Sá, Ana Lúcia, and Olivio Kilumbo. 2024. "UNITA's Post-War Parliamentary Elite." *Journal of Southern African Studies*, October 50(4): 1–20.

Sanbonmatsu, Kira. 2002. "Political Parties and the Recruitment of Women to State Legislatures." *The Journal of Politics* 64(3): 791–809.

Sandino Simanca Herrera, Victoria. 2024. "From the Mountains to the Public Arena." Berghof Foundation, March 4.

Santiago, Irene M. 2015. "The Participation of Women in the Mindanao Peace Process." *UN Women*.

Schädel, Andreas, and Véronique Dudouet. 2020. *Incremental Inclusivity: A Recipe for Effective Peace Processes?* Berlin: Berghof Foundation.

Schwindt-Bayer, Leslie. 2010. *Political Power and Women's Representation in Latin America.* Oxford University Press.

Schwindt-Bayer, Leslie A. 2003. "Legislative Representation in Latin America." Thesis. The University of Arizona.

Shair-Rosenfield, Sarah, and Reed M. Wood. 2017. "Governing Well after War." *Journal of Politics* 79(3): 995–1009.

Shekhawat, Seema. 2015. "Visible in Conflict, Invisible in Peace." In *Female Combatants in Conflict and Peace*: 100–16, Springer.

Sindre, Gyda Marås. 2016a. "In Whose Interests?" *Civil Wars* 18(2): 192–213.

Sindre, Gyda Marås. 2016b. "Internal Party Democracy in Former Rebel Parties." *Party Politics* 22(4): 501–11.

Sindre, Gyda M. 2019. "Adapting to peacetime politics? Rebranding and ideological change in former rebel parties." *Government and Opposition* 54(3), 485–512.

Söderberg Kovacs, Mimmi, and Sophia Hatz. 2016. "Rebel-to-Party Transformations in Civil War Peace Processes 1975–2011." *Democratization* 23(6): 990–1008.

Spears, Ian S. 2000. "Understanding Inclusive Peace Agreements in Africa: The Problems of Sharing Power." *Third World Quarterly* 21(1): 105–18.

Stallman, Heidi, and Falak Hadi. 2024. "Gender Inclusion and Rebel Strategy: Legitimacy Seeking Behavior in Rebel Groups." *International Politics* 62: 291–317.

Stedman, Stephen John. 1997. "Spoiler Problems in Peace Processes." *International Security* 22(2): 5–53.

Stedman, Stephen John. 2001. *Implementing Peace Agreements in Civil Wars.* New York: International Peace Academy.

Stedman, Stephen John, Donald Rothchild, and Elizabeth Cousens. 2002. *Ending Civil Wars.* Lynne Rienner.

Storm, Lise. 2020. "Exploring Post-Rebel Parties in Power: Political Space and Implications for Islamist Inclusion and Moderation." *Open Journal of Political Science* 10(04): 638–67. https://doi.org/10.4236/ojps.2020.104038.

Tamaru, Nanako, and Marie O'Reilly. 2018. "How Women Influence Constitution Making after Conflict and Unrest." *Research Report.*

Thomas, Jakana. 2014. "Rewarding Bad Behavior." *American Journal of Political Science* 58(4): 804–18.

Thomas, Jakana L. 2023. "Sisters Are Doing It for Themselves." *American Political Science Review* 118(2), 831–47.

Tønnessen, Liv, and Samia al-Nagar. 2013. "The Women's Quota in Conflict Ridden Sudan: Ideological Battles for and against Gender Equality." *Women's Studies International Forum* 41: 122–31.

Tripp, Aili. 2015. *Women and Power in Post-Conflict Africa*. Cambridge University Press.

Tripp, Aili Mari. 2016. "Women's Movements and Constitution Making after Civil Unrest and Conflict in Africa." *Politics and Gender* 12(1): 78–106.

True, Jacqui, and Yolanda Riveros-Morales. 2019. "Towards Inclusive Peace." *International Political Science Review* 40(1): 23–40.

UN Women. 2018. "Women's Meaningful Participation in Negotiating Peace." "As 8-Year Mark of Colombia's Peace Agreement Nears, Speakers in Security Council Highlight Women's Role in Driving Implementation." United Nations Security Council (UNSC). October 15, 2024.

US State Department. 2019. "Angola 2019 Human Rights Report."

Verge, Tània, and Sílvia Claveria. 2018. "Gendered Political Resources." *Party Politics* 24(5): 536–48.

Verjee, Aly. 2020. *After the Agreement*. Washington, DC: United States Institute of Peace.

Walter, Barbara. 2002. *Committing to Peace*. Princeton University Press.

Walter, Barbara F. 1997. "The Critical Barrier to Civil War Settlement." *International Organization* 51(3): 335–64.

Walter, Barbara F. 2009. "Bargaining Failures and Civil War." *Annual Review of Political Science* 12: 243–61. https://doi.org/10.1177/0022343313512853.

Waylen, Georgina. 2014. "A Seat at the Table – Is It Enough?" *Politics & Gender* 10(04): 495–523.

Webster, Kaitlyn, Chong Chen, and Kyle Beardsley. 2019. "Conflict, Peace, and the Evolution of Women's Empowerment." *International Organization* 73: 255–89.

Weeks, Ana Catalano. 2018. "Why Are Gender Quota Laws Adopted by Men?" *Comparative Political Studies* 51(14): 1935–73.

Weeks, Ana Catalano, Bonnie M. Meguid, Miki Caul Kittilson, and Hilde Coffé. 2023. "When Do Männerparteien Elect Women?" *American Political Science Review* 117(2): 421–38.

Werner, Suzanne. 1999. "The Precarious Nature of Peace." *American Journal of Political Science* 43(3): 912–34.

Wolbrecht, Christina, and David E. Campbell. 2007. "Leading by Example." *American Journal of Political Science* 51(4): 921–39.

Wood, Reed. 2019. *Female Fighters*. Columbia University Press.

Wood, Reed M., and Jakana L. Thomas. 2017. "Women on the Frontline." *Journal of Peace Research* 54(1): 31–46.

World Bank. 2023. World Development Indicators. Retrieved from data.worldbank.org/indicator/DT.ODA.ALLD.KD.

World Bank. 2024. GDP per capita (current US$). World Bank Open Data. Retrieved October 15, 2025, from data.worldbank.org/indicator/NY.GDP.PCAP.CD.

Zartman, William. 2005. "Ripeness: The Hurting Stalemate and Beyond." In *International Conflict Resolution after the Cold War*. Druckman, Daniel, and Paul C. Stern, (Eds.) 225–250 Committee on International Conflict Resolution.

Gender and Politics

Tiffany D. Barnes
University of Texas at Austin
Tiffany D. Barnes is Professor of Political Science at the University of Texas at Austin. She is the author of *Women, Politics, and Power: A Global Perspective* (Rowman & Littlefield, 2007) and, award-winning, *Gendering Legislative Behavior* (Cambridge University Press, 2016). Her research has been funded by the National Science Foundation (NSF) and recognized with numerous awards. Barnes is the former president of the Midwest Women's Caucus and founder and director of the Empirical Study of Gender (EGEN) network.

Diana Z. O'Brien
Washington University in St. Louis
Diana Z. O'Brien is the Bela Kornitzer Distinguished Professor of Political Science at Washington University in St. Louis. She specializes in the causes and consequences of women's political representation. Her award-winning research has been supported by the NSF and published in leading political science journals. O'Brien has also served as a Fulbright Visiting Professor, an associate editor at *Politics & Gender*, the president of the Midwest Women's Caucus, and a founding member of the EGEN network.

About the Series

From campaigns and elections to policymaking and political conflict, gender pervades every facet of politics. Elements in Gender and Politics features carefully theorized, empirically rigorous scholarship on gender and politics. The Elements both offer new perspectives on foundational questions in the field and identify and address emerging research areas.

Cambridge Elements

Gender and Politics

Elements in the Series

Counter-Stereotypes and Attitudes Toward Gender and LGBTQ Equality
Jae-Hee Jung and Margit Tavits

The Politics of Bathroom Access and Exclusion in the United States
Sara Chatfield

Women, Gender, and Rebel Governance during Civil Wars
Meredith Maloof Loken

Abortion Attitudes and Polarization in the American Electorate
Erin C. Cassese, Heather L. Ondercin and Jordan Randall

Gender, Ethnicity, and Intersectionality in Cabinets: Asia and Europe in Comparative Perspective
Amy H. Liu, Roman Hlatky, Keith Padraic Chew, Eoin L. Power, Sam Selsky, Betty Compton and Meiying Xu

Gendered Jobs and Local Leaders: Women, Work, and the Pipeline to Local Political Office
Rachel Bernhard and Mirya R. Holman

What's Happened to the Gender Gap in Political Activity: Social Structure, Politics, and Participation in the United States
Shauna L. Shames, Sara Morell, Ashley Jardina, Kay Lehman Schlozman and Nancy Burns

Family Matters: How Romantic Partners Shape Politicians' Careers
Olle Folke, Moa Frödin Gruneau and Johanna Rickne

Glass Ceilings, Glass Cliffs, and Quicksands: Gendered Party Leadership in Parliamentary Systems
Andrea S. Aldrich and Zeynep Somer-Topcu

Attitudes toward Political Authoritarianism in Economically Advanced Democracies: The Role of Gender Values and Norms
Amy C. Alexander and Gefjon Off

Public Preferences, Gender, and Foreign Support for Armed Movements
Çağlayan Başer

Legislating Peace: How Gender Diverse Rebel Parties Encourage the Implementation of Gender Peace Agreement Provisions
Elizabeth L. Brannon and Jakana Thomas

A full series listing is available at: www.cambridge.org/EGAP

For EU product safety concerns, contact us at Calle de José Abascal, 56–1°,
28003 Madrid, Spain or eugpsr@cambridge.org.

www.ingramcontent.com/pod-product-compliance
Lightning Source LLC
LaVergne TN
LVHW011849060526
838200LV00054B/4246